Intersectionality and Discrimination

Roger White

Intersectionality and Discrimination

An Examination of the U.S. Labor Market

palgrave
macmillan

Roger White
Whittier, CA, USA

ISBN 978-3-031-26124-4 ISBN 978-3-031-26125-1 (eBook)
https://doi.org/10.1007/978-3-031-26125-1

Cover illustration: © Harvey Loake

This Palgrave Macmillan imprint is published by the registered company Springer Nature Switzerland AG
The registered company address is: Gewerbestrasse 11, 6330 Cham, Switzerland

For Frank Patti, to whom I owe a tremendous debt of gratitude.

Acknowledgments

I am grateful to the administration of Whittier College for their continued funding of my research efforts. Accordingly, I acknowledge the generous research support provided by the Douglas W. Ferguson Chair in International Economics.

I am indebted to several individuals without whose contributions and support the completion of this book would not have been possible. I owe a debt of thanks to Lindley Lee-Niegas (Whittier College '22) for her excellent research assistance on this and several earlier projects. Lindley is an exceptional talent, and I look forward to her future endeavors and accomplishments. I would be remiss if I did not acknowledge the support and assistance of Meera Seth (Commissioning Editor), and Hemapriya Eswanth (Project Coordinator), Jayalakshmi Raju (Project Manager), and their colleagues at Palgrave Macmillan. Thank you very much.

Lastly, I owe extraordinary thanks to Michelle Espaldon for her continued friendship, never-ending patience, loving support, and companionship, and to Scout for always being the best puppy in the world.

Contents

Abbreviations

ACS	American Community Survey
ANES	American National Election Studies
BLS	Bureau of Labor Statistics
CPS	Current Population Survey
EEOC	Equal Employment Opportunity Commission

List of Figures

List of Tables

Part I

CHAPTER 1

A Rationale for the Study of Intersectional Wage Discrimination

Abstract We begin with a brief discussion of the relationship between social justice and economic justice. This is followed by a presentation of persistent differences in U.S. labor market outcomes. Specifically, we identify significant differences in unemployment rates and hourly wages across race- and sex-based classifications, respectively. We then present unadjusted wage gaps (i.e., raw differences in average hourly wage rates) for several worker groups that correspond to the non-productive personal characteristics we consider in this study. These characteristics include Hispanic ethnicity, nativity, race, and sex. Having motivated our study, we introduce intersectionality and our primary research question: Is wage discrimination intersectional? This is followed by a discussion of why we use the term "discrimination" when referring to differences in wage rates that cannot be explained by differences in workers' productive characteristics. We conclude the chapter with a roadmap for the remainder of the book.

Keyword Discrimination · Economic justice · Intersectionality · Multiple intersecting identities · Social justice · Wage gap

R. White, *Intersectionality and Discrimination*,
https://doi.org/10.1007/978-3-031-26125-1_1

In recent years, issues related to the broader topic of social justice have become increasingly prominent in the public discourse of the United States. In simple terms, social justice is focused on the extent to which fairness is exhibited in society. It emphasizes equal opportunities across individuals as well as equal economic, political, and social rights. Social justice is closely related to and is often said to encompass economic justice, which can be described as the creation of opportunities that allow individuals to establish the material foundations that are necessary for the support of creative, dignified, and productive lives. Greater economic justice requires equity in labor market processes and outcomes. This, in turn, requires fairness in employment and wage setting so that an individual can have a job that pays a living wage, have access to a quality education and affordable childcare, and be able to afford a roof over their head and food for their family.

In the U.S. labor market, economic injustice often involves discrimination that is based on personal characteristics such as age, ethnicity, race, sex, etc. Unfortunately, such inequities are often significant in magnitude and persistent over time. Two examples illustrate this point. First, regarding employment, during the past several decades, the unemployment rate for black Americans has typically been about twice the level of the white unemployment rate. Specifically, during the past half-century, the average monthly black unemployment rate has been 11.6% while the white unemployment rate has averaged only 5.5% (BLS 2022).[1] Second, in 1980, the median hourly wage of female workers in the United States was only 64% of the median wage paid to their male counterparts (Barroso and Brown 2021). Although this wage gap narrowed to 84% in 2020 (ACS 2022a), a 16% difference in median hourly wage rates across sexes is quite sizeable. In both cases, some portion of the disparity between the worker groups and their counterparts, who are white and male, respectively, may be the result of differences in productive characteristics such as education, skills, and experience. Of course, it is also possible that some, and potentially all, of the unadjusted wage gap is attributable to discrimination.

[1] Monthly unemployment rates by race are available from the U.S. Bureau of Labor Statistics (BLS). Our calculations are made using seasonally adjusted monthly unemployment rate series for the period from January 1972 through October 2022. Appendix Fig. 1.5 illustrates the striking persistence of differences between the two series.

A different type of example is found in the opening passage of Cain's (1986) survey of the literature on labor market discrimination. The paper begins as follows:

> This survey of the economics of labor market discrimination is motivated by two fundamental problems associated with income and wage differences among groups classified by sex, race, ethnicity, and other characteristics. The first is the inequity of long-lasting differences in economic well-being among the groups; in particular, differences in household or family income. The second is the inequity of long-lasting differences in the average wage rates among groups of workers classified by these demographic traits, when the groups may be presumed to be either equally productive or to have equal productive capacity. (p. 693)

It is startling just how well these words describe present conditions in the U.S. labor market. If a reader was unaware that Cain's survey was published thirty-five years ago, they could easily be forgiven for thinking the words are from a recent work. That this decades-old depiction of economic injustices remains applicable today further illustrates the persistence of inequities in the U.S. labor market.

In this work, we examine multiple topics that are related to wage discrimination.[2] We study the period from 2008 through 2020 using annual data from the American Community Survey (ACS) (2022a). We estimate wage discrimination rates for each year in our reference period for each of 43 worker groups that are defined by workers' non-productive personal characteristics (i.e., Hispanic ethnicity, nativity,

[2] While there are many other forms of labor market discrimination, our analysis is purposely limited to wage discrimination. We do not examine hiring discrimination or terminations that result from disparate treatment. We also do not examine customer discrimination (i.e., discrimination that occurs when employers internalize their customers' prejudices against workers with certain personal characteristics and, thus, demonstrate bias/prejudice against those same workers to increase profits). However, given that our focus is on wage discrimination, our data set includes employed individuals which permits us to potentially capture wage discrimination that is related to job promotions, employee discrimination, and (if wage-related) job assignments.

race,[3] and sex).[4,5] We also consider whether variation in our estimated discrimination rates follows a pattern that suggests wage discrimination is intersectional. To formally examine whether wage discrimination is intersectional, we construct expected discrimination rates for each of the worker groups that differ from our null cohort of native-born, non-Hispanic, white, male workers in two or more personal characteristics. The expected discrimination rates are compared to our estimated discrimination rates to determine whether wage discrimination is additive or non-additive (i.e., intersectional). Lastly, for each worker group, we explore possible pre-labor market wage discrimination with respect to the returns to education and whether there is overlap in affected worker groups across pre-market discrimination and intersectional wage discrimination.

1.1 Illustrating Unadjusted Wage Gaps

A brief review of unadjusted wage gaps between several worker groups during the past four-plus decades offers additional motivation for our analysis.[6] Figures 1.1 and 1.2 illustrate unadjusted wage gaps. In both figures, the average wage rates are presented relative to corresponding null worker cohorts. For example, female workers' average hourly wages

[3] Using the ACS variable RAC1, we construct six race classifications. The RAC1 variable includes nine race classifications. We merge the "American Indian alone," "Alaska native alone," and "American Indian and Alaska native tribes specified; or American Indian or Alaska native, not specified and no other races" to form a single American Indian and Alaska native classification. Likewise, we merge the "Asian alone" and the "Native Hawaiian and Other Pacific Islander alone" classifications to form a single Asian or Pacific Islander classification. Our other race classifications are "White alone," "Black or African American alone," "Some other race alone," and "Two or more major race groups," which we refer to as white, black, other race, and multiple races, respectively.

[4] Since this work examines survey data, all individual characteristics are self-identified (e.g., individuals' Hispanic ethnicity, nativity, and race classifications and their self-reported binary interpretation of sex).

[5] Throughout this work, we refer to sex-based discrimination rather than gender-based discrimination. The Census Bureau (2022a) explains that, in the ACS questionnaire, "the sex question wording very specifically intends to capture a person's biological sex and not gender." Since gender is how a person identifies and the ACS does not solicit information on gender identity, we believe that, in this work, "sex-based discrimination" is more accurate than "gender-based discrimination."

[6] Throughout this section, our discussion is focused on unadjusted wage gaps. The qualifier "unadjusted" indicates that the wage gaps identify differences in mean hourly

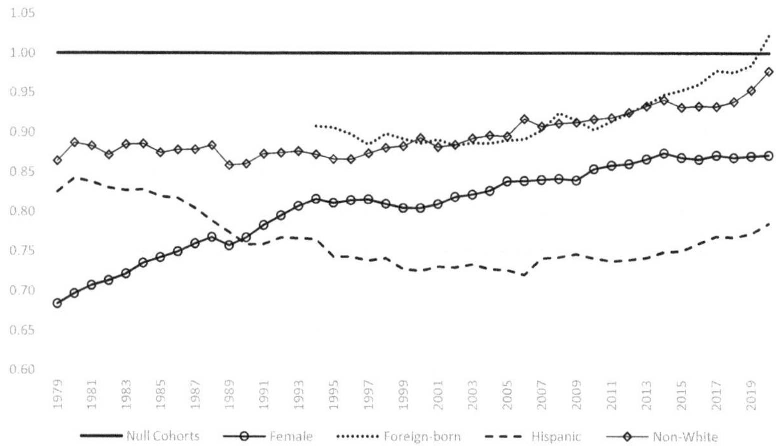

Fig. 1.1 Wage gaps by year—various worker groups: CPS data, 1979–2020 (*Source* Author's calculations based on data from the annual CPS Merged Outgoing Rotation Files [NBER 2022])

are presented relative to the average wage of male workers (i.e., the null cohort). Similarly, the average hourly wage rates of foreign-born workers, Hispanic workers, and non-white workers are presented relative to the mean hourly wage rates of their respective null cohorts: native-born workers, non-Hispanic workers, and non-white workers.[7] For each of these worker groups, the average hourly wage of the corresponding null cohort is depicted by the horizontal line that is set at the value of one. Thus, the values illustrated in the figure compare the average wage rate for each worker group to the average wage rate of the relevant null worker cohort. For example, in Fig. 1.1, we see that on average in 1989, non-white workers earned an hourly wage rate equal to 86.4% of the rate paid to white workers.

wage rates between worker groups without accounting for differences in personal characteristics that may explain variation in workers' productivity levels and, hence, affect the wage gaps.

[7] Appendix Table 1.1 provides period-specific average hourly wage rates and wage gaps for the worker cohorts that are presented in Figs. 1.1 and 1.2.

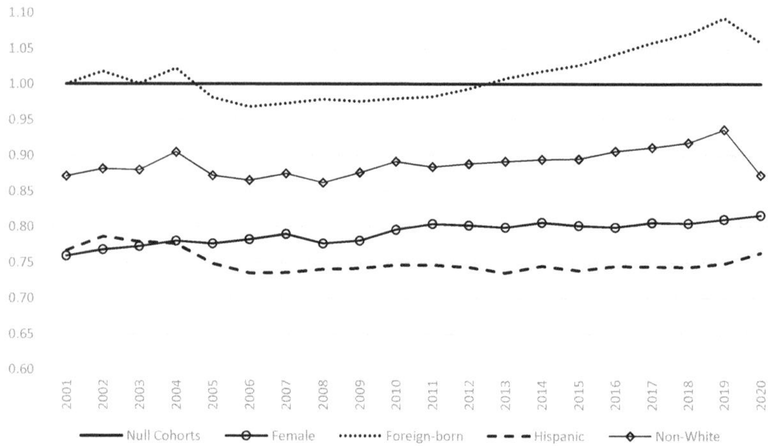

Fig. 1.2 Wage gaps by year—various worker groups: ACS data, 2001–2020 (*Source* Author's calculations based on data from annual ACS data [Census 2022])

The values illustrated in Fig. 1.1 have been calculated using data from the U.S. Current Population Survey (CPS).[8,9] We see that, on average, in 1979–1980 female workers were paid nearly 31% less per hour than their male counterparts. In more recent years, this wage gap has diminished, falling to 19.3% during the 1991–2000 period, and reaching 13.3% during the decade since 2010.[10] Similar patterns of diminished wage gaps are found for other worker groups. For example, the gap in average hourly wage rates between non-white and white workers remained largely

[8] Specifically, the calculations are made using CPS Merged Outgoing Rotation Group Earnings Data available from the National Bureau of Economic Research (2022).

[9] While the CPS data are available for a lengthier period than the ACS data, we limit our analysis to the evaluation of ACS data during the 2008–2020 period. This is the result of two factors. First, there are differences in the measurement of educational attainment in the ACS data before 2008 relative to more recent years. Second, CPS sample sizes for some worker groups (i.e., American Indian and Alaska native, Asian or Pacific Islander, and those who identify as being of multiple races) are so small that we cannot identify members of several race cohorts in earlier years.

[10] The average values presented are the mean annual unadjusted wage gaps. They are not weighted by annual sample sizes.

constant at approximately 12% from 1979 to 1980 through the 1991–2000 period before falling by roughly one-half to an average value of 5.9% during the 2011–2020 period.[11] Although data are only available for an abbreviated period, we observe a similar pattern for foreign-born workers and their native-born counterparts. By contrast, however, when differences in average wage rates between Hispanic workers and non-Hispanic workers are calculated, we do not see a decrease in the wage gap across time. Instead, we see an initial increase in the gap that is followed in the most recent three decade-length periods by gaps of near equal magnitudes.

To provide additional information, and as something of a check against the wage gaps we have generated using CPS data, we also calculate wage gaps using data from the ACS.[12] These values are presented in Fig. 1.2. ACS data are only available since 2001, thus the time period is abbreviated (Census 2022b, c). We find that the average wage values generated from ACS data are generally higher than those calculated using CPS data. Even so, across the two data sources, the proportional wage gaps for most worker groups are quite similar in terms of their magnitudes and the directions of change over time. Consistent with the values obtained when examining CPS data, calculations made using ACS data identify a slight downward trend in wage gaps over time for female workers, non-white workers, and foreign-born workers. In fact, it appears that foreign-born workers have, on average, already achieved parity with native-born workers. There also are some signs of convergence between other worker groups and their respective comparison cohorts. Even so, both figures illustrate several significant and persistent wage gaps, and in both figures, we see divergence with respect to the unadjusted wage gap for Hispanic workers.

The persistence of the wage gaps we have presented can be further illustrated through a few "back of the envelope" calculations. In Fig. 1.1, the trend annual decrease in the male-female wage gap during the 1979–2020 period is 0.42 percentage points. A linear extrapolation using this

[11] Due to CPS data limitations, nativity-based wage gaps cannot be calculated for years before 1994.

[12] Although hourly wage rates are provided in the CPS, to include both hourly-paid and salaried workers, from both the CPS and ACS, hourly wage rates are inferred from annual salary amounts divided by the product of the typical hours worked per week and the number of weeks worked during the past year.

value suggests that female-male wage parity will be achieved in 2048. This is 26 years into the future (i.e., about one full generation). Based on the ACS data (i.e., values presented in Fig. 1.2), male-female wage parity will not be achieved until 2096 (i.e., 74 years, or about three generations, into the future). Similarly, based on the CPS data, non-white workers will achieve parity with white workers in 31 years. Again, based on the ACS data, parity between these two groups will occur in 50 years. As noted, for Hispanic workers, in both figures, the linear trend is moving away from parity.[13]

1.2 Why Intersectionality?

A straightforward definition of wage discrimination is paying equally productive workers unequal amounts due to differences in the workers' ages, ethnicities, nativities, races, sexes, or other protected characteristic(s).[14] As we have shown, in the U.S. labor market, there are persistent and sizeable differences in average wage rates across broadly defined worker groups. Unfortunately, even as the economics literature robustly reports findings that are consistent with wage discrimination, the personal characteristics by which individuals suffer discrimination have almost always been viewed in isolation.[15] For example, Ganji (2019), Banerjee et al. (2018), and Wang et al. (2017) explore sex-based wage differentials, hiring discrimination based on perceived race, and wage differentials between native- and foreign-born cohorts, respectively. Each of these studies considers discrimination related to a single personal characteristic. This is problematic since it is quite reasonable to presume that workers may simultaneously suffer discrimination related to multiple personal

[13] To emphasize, these are very simple calculations. Of course, there is no guarantee that gaps will narrow at all or that, if convergence does occur, it will follow an extrapolated path. Remember, we present these values to demonstrate the persistence of wage gaps across time.

[14] The U.S. Equal Employment Opportunity Commission identifies age (40 years and older), disability, genetic information/family medical history, nativity/national origin, race/color, religion, and sex (i.e., gender identity, pregnancy, and sexual orientation) as protected characteristics with respect to labor market discrimination (EEOC 2022). Owing to limited data availability, our analysis considers only the characteristics of Hispanic ethnicity, nativity, race, and sex.

[15] See Cain (1986), Altonji and Blank (1999), Lang and Lehmann (2011), and Neumark (2018) for detailed surveys of the related literature.

characteristics. Likewise, it may be that workers' multiple intersecting identities interact to create unique levels of discrimination.

To be sure, measuring disparate treatment in the labor market is not as straightforward as some may believe. Setting aside any discussion of empirical techniques for the moment, on a base level, quantifying discrimination is a difficult task. For example, given the differences in unemployment rates across races and the differences in average wages across sexes that have been noted, one may reasonably conclude that the typical black female worker, being potentially subjected to both race-based and sex-based discrimination, may more likely be unemployed or earn less per hour relative to the typical white male worker. This certainly seems a reasonable expectation, but would the discrimination suffered by a black woman be equivalent to the sum of discrimination that is based on her sex and the discrimination that is based on her race (i.e., the combination of discrimination faced by a white woman and by a black man)?[16] Or might it be that, due to their specific intersecting identities, black women face discrimination that is separate and distinct (i.e., non-additive discrimination)?[17]

The notion of non-additive effects, as considered in relation to wage discrimination, aligns with the concept of intersectionality. Crenshaw (1989, 1991) coined the term "intersectionality" to describe how interdependent and overlapping systems of discrimination and disadvantage may intersect to create unique dynamics and effects. These systems of discrimination align with social categories that are based on personal characteristics and identities (e.g., nationality, race, sex, socioeconomic class, etc.). Thus, an intersectional analysis involves the examination of how multiple forms of discrimination may intersect.

Intersectional analysis has yet to gain a significant foothold in empirical economic analysis. To date, fewer than a handful of studies examine discrimination in the U.S. labor market from an intersectional perspective. Much to the contrary, substantial inroads have been made in other disciplines. Bauer et al. (2021) provide a meta-analysis of more than 700 peer-reviewed articles that have applied intersectional frameworks and have been published during the past 30 years. The authors report that

[16] Greenman and Xie (2008) appropriately refer to this as "the additive assumption."

[17] Berthoud (2003) and Watson and Lunn (2010) both propose that, given multiple identities and relative to any single identity, wage discrimination may be additive, multiplicative, or subtractive.

a large majority of the studies (83.2%) were published in journals focused on four disciplines: Psychology (24% of the total), Sociology (23.1%), Medical and Life Science (21.2%), and Gender and Sexuality (14.9%). Only 4.1% of the articles were published in Business and Economics journals and none of these works examine wage discrimination. The work presented here extends the economics literature by providing the first comprehensive intersectional study of wage discrimination in the U.S. labor market.

Before moving forward, with the hope of providing clarity and because it is not uncommon for certain terms to be used in ways that support normative agendas (Collins 2015), it is important to specify what we mean when using the terms "intersectional" and "intersectionality." Crenshaw, when asked in 2020 to explain what intersectionality means today, offered the following response:

> These days, I start with what it's not, because there has been distortion. It's not identity politics on steroids. It is not a mechanism to turn white men into the new pariahs. It's basically a lens, a prism, for seeing the way in which various forms of inequality often operate together and exacerbate each other. We tend to talk about race inequality as separate from inequality based on gender, class, sexuality or immigrant status. What's often missing is how some people are subject to all of these, and the experience is not just the sum of its parts. (Steinmetz 2020)

Consistent with Crenshaw's response, we examine possible wage discrimination for a large number of groups that are defined based on the worker's multiple intersecting identities.[18] As noted, the specific personal characteristics we consider include Hispanic ethnicity, nativity, race, and sex. Given that the ACS data set allows for the identification of respondents into six race classifications and each of the remaining three identities is

[18] Note that the goal of this work is not to convince anyone that wage discrimination exists in America. A large body of empirical research documents unexplained wage gaps across worker cohorts defined by group characteristics; thus, we accept that wage discrimination exists.

binary, our analysis includes as many as 44 distinct worker groups identified by their multiple intersecting identities.[19,20] We designate workers who are native-born, non-Hispanic, white, and male as our null worker cohort. Figure 1.3 illustrates the intersection of multiple identities for the null worker cohort and each of the comparison groups.[21]

To estimate the extent of wage discrimination, each worker group is compared to the null worker cohort, in turn, for each of the 13 years in our reference period. This involves estimating a series of augmented Mincer earnings functions and Heckman sample selection models and the use of the Blinder-Oaxaca decomposition technique. The result is a series of annual estimates of wage discrimination.[22] To determine whether wage discrimination is intersectional (i.e., non-additive), for each worker group that differs from our null worker cohort in two or more of the four personal characteristics considered, we compare our estimated wage discrimination rate to an expected discrimination rate (i.e., an additive measure) that is constructed as the sum of characteristic-specific discrimination rates. If the estimated and expected discrimination rates values are comparable (i.e., the values differ by no more than five percentage points), then wage discrimination is considered to be additive and, thus, not intersectional. If, however, the values differ by more than five percentage points, then the wage discrimination is intersectional (i.e., non-additive).

[19] Given that we examine six race classifications and that the Hispanic ethnicity, nativity, and sex characteristics are binary, there are 48 potential worker groups to examine. We limit our study to 44 worker groups by excluding observations that report being both foreign-born (i.e., an immigrant) and American Indian and Alaska native. This results in four worker group classifications being excluded from the analysis: foreign-born, non-Hispanic, American Indian and Alaska native, male workers; foreign-born, non-Hispanic, American Indian and Alaska native, female workers; native-born, non-Hispanic, American Indian and Alaska native, male workers; and native-born, non-Hispanic, American Indian and Alaska native, female workers.

[20] Insufficient data sometimes result in fewer than 44 worker groups being examined. Specifically, in a given year, we exclude worker groups from our analysis if the sample size of the group is less than 250 observations.

[21] The figure identifies eight combinations of overlapping identities. Identical diagrams can be produced for each of the six race classifications in the ACS.

[22] Given that we employ the Mincer equation, we are also able to examine variation in returns to formal education (i.e., possible pre-labor market discrimination) across the worker groups.

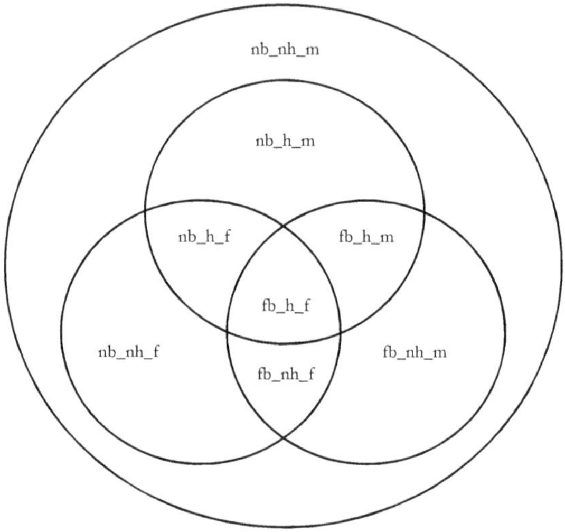

Fig. 1.3 Illustrating multiple intersecting identities (*Note* Ethnicity [h = Hispanic, nh = non-Hispanic], Nativity [fb = foreign-born, nb = native-born)], Sex [f = female, m = male])

1.3 Why Say "Discrimination"?

The existence and persistence of large and unexplained differences in labor market outcomes are often presented as indirect evidence of potential labor market discrimination. Viewing these differences as circumstantial evidence of discrimination is a conservative, although admittedly accurate, interpretation. Statistical analysis may suggest but cannot definitively confirm that discrimination has occurred. When results suggest discrimination has occurred, the extent of the discriminatory behavior can only be estimated. Consequently, researchers are generally cautious when interpreting, say, an unexplained wage gap or some other seemingly disparate treatment. Although this careful approach is understandable given the limitations of data and empirical analysis, such an approach may not be advisable or even responsible when addressing such an important issue. In fact, adopting a cautious approach may understate the extent of the unequal treatment and, if so, risk de-emphasizing the problem. D'Amico (1987) correctly and succinctly stresses the broad societal implications of research into potential labor market discrimination when writing:

> The labor market does not stand alone, insulated from the society at large. Rather, these markets are nestled into society, processing and filtering the prevailing customs and political and social arrangements and translating these into particular, tangible economic outcomes. These outcomes, therefore, reflect more than just the organizational and technical characteristics of production and the resource endowments of the individual and society. Market outcomes reflect social relations and feed back on them, and nowhere is the importance of this interaction more pronounced than in the dynamics of discrimination. (p. 132)

Even though a conservative interpretation of results may be justified based on a desire to avoid reaching conclusions that may not be fully supported by the data, there is ample evidence of discrimination in the United States. Direct evidence of racial bias is found in the American National Election Studies data set (ANES 2021). In each presidential election year since 1964, ANES interviewers have read the following statement to survey respondents:

> We'd also like to get your feelings about some groups in American society. When I read the name of a group, we'd like you to rate it with what we call a feeling thermometer. Ratings between 50 degrees-100 degrees mean that you feel favorably and warm toward the group; ratings between 0 and 50 degrees mean that you don't feel favorably towards the group and that you don't care too much for that group. If you don't feel particularly warm or cold toward a group you would rate them at 50 degrees. If we come to a group you don't know much about, just tell me and we'll move on to the next one.

Respondents are then asked to express their feelings toward several groups, including broad racial classifications. Additionally, in response to a separate question, ANES respondents indicate their race. So, each respondent indicates their race, their feelings toward their race, and their feelings toward other races. Considering only those respondents who identify as white and evaluating their feelings toward both whites and blacks, we construct a time-varying estimate of white bias against blacks in the United States. Figure 1.4 illustrates.

The solid line in the figure represents the average difference across white ANES respondents in terms of their reported feeling thermometer values for whites and blacks. For example, in 1964 the average white respondent reported their feelings toward other whites as 85.52 on the

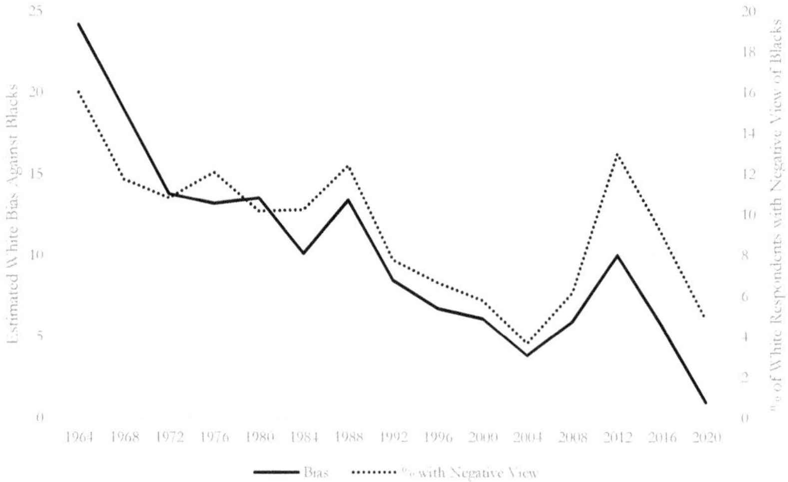

Fig. 1.4 Estimated white bias against blacks, 1964–2020 (*Source* Author's calculations based on data from the ANES [2021])

0–100 scale and their feelings toward blacks as 61.32. Thus, the estimated white bias (measured along the left y-axis in the figure) for 1964 is equal to 24.2. With few exceptions, the trend in white bias values has been downward. In 2004, the value was only 3.83, and the average white feeling thermometer value for blacks exceeded 70 for the first time. Following increases in estimated white bias values during 2008 and 2012, the series again decreased, registering its lowest value (0.95) in 2020. A different measure, the percentage of white respondents who reported having a negative view of blacks, is measured along the right y-axis in the figure. Here, a negative view is defined as not feeling favorable toward or not caring too much for blacks and is indicated by a feeling thermometer value of less than 50. The series follows a path that is quite similar to the reported estimates of white bias.

Additional evidence of discrimination is found among the results of a 2017 poll administered by the Harvard T. H. Chan School of Public Health, the Robert Wood Johnson Foundation, and National Public

Radio (RWJF 2018).[23] The poll provides several striking findings. First, "50% of black Americans say they have been personally discriminated against because of their race when interacting with the police" (p. 5). Second, "[W]omen are more than twice as likely as men to report gender discrimination when it comes to equal pay or consideration for promotion (41% women vs. 18% men), and nearly twice as likely as men to report gender discrimination when applying for jobs (31% women vs. 18% men)" (p. 7).[24] Third, "Nearly half (45%) of black Americans, 31% of Latinos, and 25% of Asian Americans say they have personally experienced racial or ethnic discrimination when trying to rent a room or apartment or buy a house" (p. 11). Finally, "22% of black Americans, 17% of Latinos, and 15% of Native Americans report that they have avoided seeking medical care for themselves or a member of their family out of concern that they would be discriminated against or treated poorly because of their race, compared to 9% of Asian Americans and only 3% of whites who report this behavior" (p. 13).

Whether considering subjective perceptions of having experienced discrimination or more objective measures from which racial bias can be inferred, there is ample evidence supporting the notion that disparate treatment exists in the United States. Again, this is not a new phenomenon, and it is likely not surprising to anyone familiar with the nation's difficult history regarding race and racial equity. Acknowledging the societal context in which discrimination is being measured is arguably a more appropriate path to follow than simply adopting conservative interpretations of empirical findings based on an inability to fully separate discrimination from other causes of wage gaps. Accordingly, as noted earlier, in this work we break with convention by taking the position that it is better to attribute unexplained portions of wage gaps to discrimination and potentially overstate the extent of discrimination than risk understating discrimination and potentially diminishing the problem.

[23] Bleich et al. (2019) and Findling et al. (2019) examine survey data and report that, relative to non-Hispanic white respondents, black Americans and Latinos have higher likelihoods of reported discrimination and anticipated discrimination related to health care and police interactions. Black Americans are also found to have a higher likelihood of hearing microaggressions and racial slurs.

[24] Of particular relevance to wage discrimination, larger shares of women (41%), Asian Americans (25%), black Americans (57%), Latinos (32%), Native Americans (33%), and LGBTQ people (22%) reported experiencing bias regarding equal pay (RWJF 2018).

1.4 A Roadmap

In the next chapter, we provide context for our study of intersectional wage discrimination, we begin the chapter with detailed non-technical introductions to the two dominant economic theories of labor market discrimination: taste-based discrimination and statistical discrimination. We then review the related economic literature. This includes survey papers on the topic and thorough reviews of the three existing economic studies of intersectional wage discrimination. We close the chapter by explicitly stating our full set of research questions. In Chapter 3, we present our empirical strategy. This entails introductions to the Mincer earnings function, the Blinder-Oaxaca decomposition technique, and the Heckman two-step selection bias correction procedure. We present our battery of regression models and demonstrate our methodology via a series of estimations for broadly defined worker groups.

Having identified our research questions and empirical strategy, we present and discuss our estimated discrimination rates in Chapter 4. In Chapter 5, we calculate expected discrimination rates and compare the estimated and expected rates to determine whether wage discrimination is intersectional. We conclude our analysis with a modest application of our findings. Specifically, we consider possible evidence of pre-labor market discrimination by considering variation across worker groups in average returns to education with the identification of intersectional wage discrimination. Lastly, in Chapter 6, we close with a summary of our topic, the research questions we examine, our empirical strategy, and our results.

Appendix

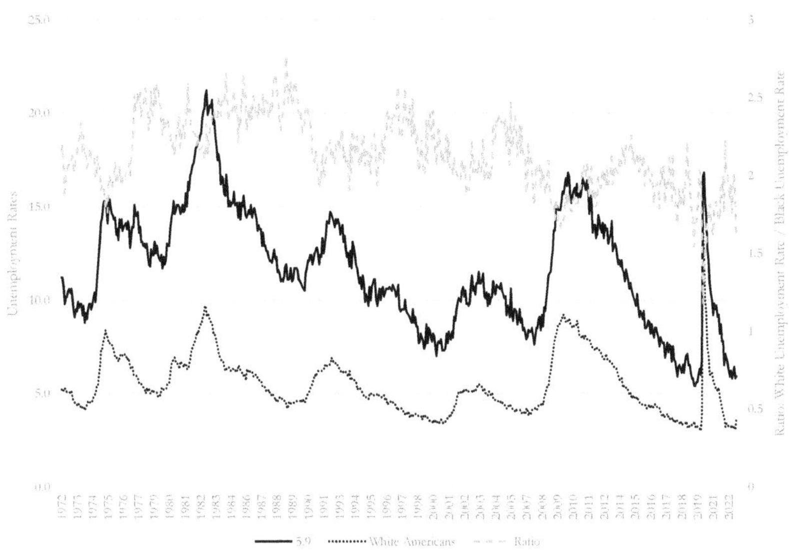

Fig. 1.5 Monthly unemployment rates—black and white workers, 1972–2022 (*Source* BLS [2022])

Table 1.1 Average wage rates and corresponding gaps, select periods, for various groups

	Data	*1979–1980*	*1981–1990*	*1991-2000*[a]	*2001–2010*	*2011–2020*
Female	CPS	5.50	8.12	12.1	17.45	22.7
Male	CPS	7.96	10.85	14.99	20.91	26.17
	%Dif	30.9%	25.2%	19.3%	16.5%	13.3%
Female	ACS				20.87	26.55
Male	ACS				26.71	32.97
	%Dif				21.9%	19.5%
Foreign-born	CPS			13.11	17.69	23.75
Native-born	CPS			14.55	19.60	24.74
	%Dif			9.9%	9.7%	4.0%
Foreign-born	ACS				23.86	31.15
Native-born	ACS				24.17	29.95
	%Dif				1.3%	–4.0%
Hispanic	CPS	5.91	7.96	10.58	14.71	19.25

(continued)

Table 1.1 (continued)

	Data	*1979–1980*	*1981–1990*	*1991-2000*[a]	*2001–2010*	*2011–2020*
Non-Hispanic	CPS	7.08	9.83	13.99	19.92	25.35
	%Dif	16.5%	19.0%	24.4%	26.2%	24.1%
Hispanic	ACS				18.65	23.33
Non-Hispanic	ACS				24.78	31.11
	%Dif				24.7%	25.0%
Non-White	CPS	6.24	8.69	12.28	17.79	23.40
White	CPS	7.12	9.88	13.96	19.64	24.86
	%Dif	12.4%	12.0%	12.0%	9.4%	5.9%
Non-White	ACS				21.71	28.07
White	ACS				24.72	30.70
	%Dif				12.2%	8.6%

[a]Due to data limitations, the average wage rates of foreign-born and native-born workers that are calculated using CPS data are only for the years 1994–2000

Note Average wage rates have been calculated using CPS and ACS population weights as appropriate

References

Altonji and Blank. 1999. Race and Gender in the Labor Market. In *Handbook of Labor Economics*, ed. Orley Ashenfelter. Amsterdam: Elsevier.

American National Election Studies (ANES). 2021. ANES Time Series Cumulative Data File [dataset and documentation]. November 18, 2021 version. www.electionstudies.org.

Banerjee, Rupa, Jeffrey G. Reitz, and Phil Oreopoulos. 2018. Do Large Employers Treat Racial Minorities More Fairly? An Analysis of Canadian Field Experiment Data. *Canadian Public Policy/Analyse De Politiques* 44 (1): 1–12.

Barroso, Amanda, and Anna Brown. 2021. "Gender Pay Gap in U.S. Held Steady in 2020". Pew Research Center. Online. https://www.pewresearch.org/?p=257386.

Bauer, Greta R., Siobhan M. Churchill, Mayuri Mahendran, Chantel Walwyn, Daniel Lizotte, and Alma Angelica Villa-Rueda. 2021. Intersectionality in Quantitative Research: A Systematic Review of its Emergence and Applications of Theory and Methods. *SSM—Population Health* 14 (6): 100798

Berthoud, Richard. 2003. *Multiple Disadvantages in Employment: A Quantitative Analysis*. London: Macdonald and Jane's.

Bleich, Sara N., Mary G. Findling, Logan S. Casey, Robert J. Blendon, John M. Benson, Gillian K. SteelFisher, Justin M. Sayde, and Carolyn Miller. 2019. Discrimination in the United States: Experiences of Black Americans. *Health Services Research* 54 (S2): 1399–1408.

Cain, Glen G. 1986. The Economic Analysis of Labor Market Discrimination: A Survey. In *Handbook of Labor Economics, Volume 1*, ed. Orley Ashenfelter and Richard Layard. Amsterdam: Elsevier.

Collins, Patricia Hill. 2015. Intersectionality's Definitional Dilemmas. *Annual Review of Sociology* 41: 1–20.

Crenshaw, Kimberle. 1989. Demarginalizing the Intersection of Race and Sex: A Black Feminist Critique of Antidiscrimination Doctrine, Feminist Theory and Antiracist Politics. University of Chicago Legal Forum: Vol. 1989, Article 8.

Crenshaw, Kimberle. 1991. Mapping the Margins: Intersectionality, Identity Politics, and Violence Against Women of Color. *Stanford Law Review* 43 (6): 1241–1299.

D'Amico, Thomas F. 1987. The Conceit of Labor Market Discrimination. *The American Economic Review: Papers and Proceedings* 77 (2): 310–315.

Findling, Mary G., Sara N. Bleich, Logan S. Casey, Robert J. Blendon, John M. Benson, Justin M. Sayde, and Carolyn Miller. 2019. Discrimination in the United States: Experiences of Latinos. *Health Services Research* 54 (S2): 1409–1418.

Ganji, Niloofar. 2019. Male-female Wage Differentials in the San Francisco Bay Area. MPRA, Paper No. 95140. Munich: University Library of Munich.

Greenman, Emily and Yu Xie. 2008. Double Jeopardy? The Interaction of Gender and Race on Earnings in the United States. *Social Forces* 86 (3): 1217–1244.

Lang, Kevin, and Jee-Yeon K. Lehmann. 2011. Racial Discrimination in the Labor Market: Theory and Empirics. NBER Working Paper No. 17450.

National Bureau of Economic Research (NBER). 2022. Current Population Survey (CPS)—Merged Outgoing Rotation Group Earnings Data. https://www.nber.org/research/data/current-population-survey-cps-merged-outgoing-rotation-group-earnings-data.

Neumark, David. 2018. Experimental Research on Labor Market Discrimination. *Journal of Economic Literature* 56 (3): 799–866.

Robert Wood Johnson Foundation/Harvard T.H. Chan School of Public Health (RWJF). 2018. Discrimination in America: Final Summary. Cambridge, MA: Harvard University. Retrieved from https://cdn1.sph.harvard.edu/wp-content/uploads/sites/94/2018/01/NPR-RWJF-HSPH-Discrimination-Final-Summary.pdf.

Steinmetz, Katy. 2020. She Coined the Term Intersectionality Over 30 Years Ago. Here's What It Means to Her Today, *Time*, February 20.

United States Bureau of Labor Statistics (BLS). 2022. Civilian Unemployment Rate, Seasonally Adjusted. U.S. Department of Labor. Retrieved from https://www.bls.gov/charts/employment-situation/civilian-unemployment-rate.htm.

United States Census Bureau (Census). 2022a. American Community Survey (ACS): Why We Ask: Sex. Retrieved from https://www2.census.gov/programs-surveys/acs/about/qbyqfact/Sex.pdf.
United States Census Bureau/American Factfinder (Census). 2022b. American Community Survey (Annual Data, 2005–2020). U.S. Census Bureau's American Community Survey Office. Retrieved from http://factfinder.census.gov.
United States Census Bureau (Census). 2022c. American Community Survey (Annual Data, 2005–2020). Retrieved from https://www.census.gov/programs-surveys/acs/technical-documentation/user-notes/2004-01.html.
United States Equal Employment Opportunity Commission (EEOC). 2022. Who Is Protected from Employment Discrimination? Retrieved from https://www.eeoc.gov/employers/small-business/3-who-protected-employment-discrimination.
Wang, Sharron Xuanren, Isao Takei, and Arthur Sakamoto. 2017. Do Asian Americans Face Labor Market Discrimination? Accounting for the Cost of Living among Native-born Men and Women. *American Sociological Association* 3: 1–14.
Watson, Dorothy and Peter Lunn. 2010. Multiple Disadvantage: Evidence on Gender and Disability from the 2006 Census. In *Making Equality Count: Irish and International Research Measuring Inequality and Discrimination*, ed. Laurence Bond, Frances McGinnity, and Helen Russell. Dublin: Liffey Press.

CHAPTER 2

Theories of Discrimination and a Review of the Related Literature

Abstract To provide context for our study of intersectional wage discrimination, we begin with detailed non-technical introductions to the two dominant economic theories of labor market discrimination: taste-based discrimination and statistical discrimination. We discuss the emotional motives for taste-based discrimination, including individual-level and contextual-level explanations for intergroup bias. In our discussion of statistical discrimination, we emphasize how imperfect information can lead a rational, profit-seeking employer to discriminate. Specifically, we focus on how experiences, generalizations, and stereotypes may lead to discrimination if employers find it difficult or impossible to predict the productivity of a potential hire or to measure the productivity of existing employees. Having provided a theoretical rationale for the existence of wage discrimination, we review the related economics literature. This includes a discussion of survey papers on the topic before more thoroughly commenting on the three existing economic studies of intersectional wage discrimination. We close this chapter by explicitly stating our full set of research questions.

Keyword Imperfect information · Intergroup bias · Literature review · Statistical discrimination · Taste-based discrimination

R. White, *Intersectionality and Discrimination*,
https://doi.org/10.1007/978-3-031-26125-1_2

In Chapter 1, we presented unadjusted wage gaps (i.e., raw differences in mean hourly wage rates) for a handful of broadly defined worker groups. In Appendix Table 1.1, for example, we reported that, based on CPS data, the average hourly wage rate for Hispanic workers during the 2011–2020 period was 24.1% less than the amount paid to non-Hispanic workers. Similarly, during the same period, female workers were paid, on average, 13.33% less than their male counterparts. These values, among others, are illustrated in Fig. 1.1. We also noted in the initial chapter that, although the unadjusted wage gaps are interesting and in some instances of considerable magnitude, they cannot be construed as an indication of wage discrimination since no accounting was made for differences in productive characteristics across worker cohorts. This is important since wage discrimination results when an employer pays a worker less than an *equally productive* worker due to their age, ethnicity, gender, nativity, race, or other protected characteristic(s).

To provide more context for our review of the literature on wage discrimination, we begin this chapter with an overview of the theoretical foundations of wage discrimination. Theoretical models are immensely important as they allow behaviors to be modeled and inferences to be made regarding otherwise unobserved behaviors (Varian 1992). The two most prominent theories of wage discrimination are taste-based discrimination (Becker 1957; Marshall 1974; Shulman 1996) and statistical discrimination (Arrow 1972; Phelps 1972; Stiglitz 1973). The theory of taste-based discrimination argues that bias related to personal characteristics is the main cause of discrimination, while the theory of statistical discrimination posits that discrimination is a rational response to uncertainty over workers' productivity levels. We discuss each theory before presenting our literature review.

It is important to note at the outset that, although there is a voluminous literature that examines wage discrimination, the vast majority of studies focus on single personal characteristics. Given our topic and, accordingly, the empirical approach that we follow, our review is largely constrained to those economic studies that approach our subject from an intersectional perspective.

2.1 Taste-Based Discrimination

Becker's (1957) theory of taste-based discrimination has dominated the literature on the discriminatory behavior of employers. Taste-based discrimination occurs when an employer holds a personal prejudice against workers of a particular group. Becker illustrated this through an example in which some white employers incur a disamenity (i.e., a psychological disutility factor) when hiring black workers (i.e., workers against which the employer is biased).[1] Effectively, this suggests a "taste" for hiring only those workers for which the employer holds no negative bias or for engaging in wage discrimination against any workers who are members of the group against which the employer is biased.

A simple example illustrates taste-based discrimination. Assume an employer is biased against Hispanic individuals. Assume further that the marginal cost of employing a non-Hispanic worker is simply the worker's wage and that this wage is $13.50 per hour. Because of the employer's bias, the marginal cost of employing an equally productive Hispanic worker is equal to the wage rate paid plus the value of the disamenity the employer experiences. The marginal costs of hiring non-Hispanic and Hispanic workers would be equal. However, because of the employer's bias, the non-Hispanic worker will be paid a wage that is greater than the non-Hispanic worker with the difference being equal to the value of the disamenity. If we further assume the value of the disamenity is equal to $1.50 per hour, then the wage rate paid to the Hispanic worker is $12.00 and the resulting wage gap will equal 11.1%.

We can see that the wage gap between non-Hispanic workers and their Hispanic counterparts increases with the employer's prejudices (i.e., with the disutility factor), eventually reaching a market wage equilibrium in which Hispanic workers are either employed by firms that discriminate less or that do not discriminate at all. A corresponding segregation would also occur where employers that choose to discriminate only hire non-Hispanic workers. The discriminating firms will incur higher labor costs and, all else equal, earn lower profits.[2] This outcome is referred to as

[1] A similar scenario would involve some employees require a premium to work with employees against whom they are biased.

[2] Note that this implies that the ability of employers to discriminate is greater in markets characterized by low levels of firm competition and reduced (or eliminated) in more competitive markets.

the static implication of Becker's model. The dynamic implication of the model is that, in the long run, in a competitive labor market, either the discriminating firms will be driven from the market and discrimination will disappear or the wage discrimination (i.e., the disutility factor) will disappear as profit-seeking behavior increases the demand for Hispanic workers (due to their lower wage cost) and, thus, places upward pressure on the group's wages.

The value of the disamenity, which in the above example represents the employer's bias against individuals of Hispanic ethnicity, is the difference in hourly wage rates paid to workers who are comparable in terms of their productive characteristics. Thus, the wage gap between non-Hispanic and Hispanic workers who are equally productive represents the extent of the employer's bias. In Becker's (1957) theory of discrimination, employers who have a taste for discrimination are identified by the action of setting a lower wage rate for members of the group they view unfavorably. In our example, employers have a taste for non-Hispanic workers and, thus, discriminate against Hispanic workers by paying them a lower wage.

Although Becker's model explains the existence of discrimination, it does not address why some employers may have this taste for discrimination. Psychologists and sociologists have studied intergroup bias, and their efforts provide useful insights which can be categorized as either individual-level or contextual-level explanations. Individual-level explanations generally suggest that taste-based discrimination in hiring and/or wage setting is the result of employers' dispositions or their negative socialization experiences. These personal dispositions or socialization experiences, especially when occurring early in life, contribute to the development of biases and prejudices that may later manifest as discrimination (Fiske 1998; Hodson and Dhont 2015). Fiske (1998) cites the authoritarian personality as an example of individual-level theory. Due to strict and punitive parenting styles, the "authoritarian" exhibits repressed aggression and fear in adulthood, eventually projecting their aggression and fear onto members of groups that differ from the "authoritarian" in terms of personal characteristics.[3]

[3] Two more recent individual-level theories are the social dominance orientation theory and the need for closure theory. The former suggests that negative bias towards members of other groups results from a desire for group-based inequality (Sidanius et al. 2004). The latter posits that negative biases stem from a need for structure/order and greater certainty in one's living environment (Kruglanski et al. 2006).

There are two prominent theories in the contextual-level category. First, conflict theory is related to competition, whether real or perceived, for scarce resources (e.g., jobs and/or earnings, promotions, social standing, etc.) and how differences in cultural norms and values between groups may lead some individuals to feel that their standards of living and their culture, respectively, are threatened (Quillian 1995; Scheepers et al. 2002). Second, contact theory holds that given certain favorable conditions are satisfied (e.g., cooperation, equality, similar goals, and support by authorities), increased contact between individuals from different groups will reduce negative biases toward members of other groups (Allport 1954; Pettigrew and Tropp 2006). Thus, contextual-level explanations are typically more dynamic than individual-level theories since they stress a fluid relationship between taste-based discrimination and the nature of intergroup relations and attitudes.

2.2 Statistical Discrimination

Phelps (1972) proposed the theory of statistical discrimination as an alternative to Becker's "taste for discrimination" model. Statistical discrimination occurs when an employer lacks information on a worker's productivity at the time of hire or when the employer is unable to accurately measure a worker's productivity once they are employed. Given this lack of information, the employer may rely on observable personal characteristics (e.g., age, gender, race, etc.) to form expectations of a worker's productivity.[4] Thus, Phelps posits that when information is asymmetric an employer's perception of reality plays an important role with respect to hiring decisions and wage setting. It is not at all uncommon for an employer to have incomplete information about the productivity of a job candidate. Resumes, references, and the interview process offer limited information to employers, and the information that is obtained may not be entirely accurate. Additionally, due to time and monetary constraints, it is often not possible to extensively assess employees. This encourages employers to find ways of minimizing the risks of overpaying their workers or making poor hiring decisions.

Arrow (1998) contends that to compensate for asymmetric information, employers inform their expectations of productivity based on their

[4] Arrow (1972), Phelps (1972), Aigner and Cain (1977), and Lundberg and Startz (1983) established the foundations of statistical discrimination.

previous experiences with individuals from groups that are comprised of similar individuals, or, worse still, employers rely on second-hand information that may include generalizations or stereotypes. Three scenarios help to illustrate this. Assume that obtaining information regarding a worker's productivity is either costly or simply not possible. Faced with limited information, the employer may rely on their prior experiences or their perceptions to infer the worker's productivity level. This may involve assuming that the new hire's productivity will equal the mean productivity of the group to which the worker belongs. If the worker is from a group that, on average, possesses less human capital than workers from other groups, the employer will rationally discriminate against the worker by either not making a job offer or paying too low a wage.[5] Similarly, the average amount of human capital may be the same across worker groups but the variance in human capital acquisition may differ from group to group. If the worker is from a group that the employer knows to have a higher variance in human capital levels, they may choose to not hire the worker or, as a hedge against a poor hiring decision, they may opt to pay too low a wage (Aigner and Cain 1977). Finally, if the employer has had limited contact with the group of which the new hire is a member they may base their expectations of productivity levels on negative stereotypes they have heard about members of that group (e.g., that members are lazy or unreliable). Using generalizations to reduce the information asymmetry and, thus, ascribing the perceived group characteristics to the individual and choosing not to hire or setting too low a wage is statistical discrimination.

While statistical discrimination is consistent with the rational, profit-maximizing behavior that is expected from firms, it is also based on prejudicial beliefs or stereotypes about a group. In fact, contrary to the irrational, emotional motives for discrimination that are assumed to exist in the taste-based model, the theory of statistical discrimination posits that imperfect information can result in labor market discrimination even when employers are rational profit-maximizers (Arrow 1972, 1998; Phelps 1972). It is also noteworthy that, unlike taste-based discrimination, where an individual's prejudices and biases underlie inequitable

[5] Audit study interviews with employers reveal that black workers are often less likely to be hired because employers perceive them as being less skilled/productive or as having less desirable work habits relative to other workers (Moss and Tilly 2001; Kirschenman and Neckerman 1991).

treatment, statistical discrimination is situational. Circumstances such as uncertainty associated with asymmetric information largely determine whether discrimination occurs. Thus, the extent of statistical discrimination declines as more accurate information becomes available to the employer.

2.3 A Review of the Related Literature

Due to strong and sustained interest in labor market discrimination among researchers—perhaps a direct result (and indicative) of the persistence of unexplained earnings gaps—a considerable literature on the topic has emerged during the past several decades. Not surprisingly, periodically, survey papers have been published to summarize and organize recent contributions in ways that add understanding to the larger body of works. We chronicle these surveys before shifting our focus to individual research efforts.[6]

Cain (1986) and D'Amico (1987) provide the earliest surveys of the literature on labor market discrimination. Given that these surveys were written approximately three decades after Becker (1957) presented his model of taste-based discrimination and fewer than 15 years after Arrow (1972) and Phelps (1972) introduced statistical discrimination, it is not surprising that the surveys provided by Cain and D'Amico focus more on studies of taste-based discrimination. Cain includes an excellent discussion of what is meant by the term "economic discrimination" and provides an especially detailed review of the empirical literature. D'Amico offers both a comprehensive review of the literature and an impressively critical discussion of empirical efforts to test the predictions of Becker's model. In subsequent years, advances were realized in the theoretical foundations of labor market discrimination and the empirical methods used to examine the topic. These advances are reflected in Altonji and Blank (1999) which provides an expansive review of studies of race-based and gender-based discrimination while also offering discussions of the efficacy of anti-discrimination policies and of how differences in pre-market human capital (e.g., education, experience, training, etc.) may affect labor market outcomes.

[6] Given the large literature on labor market discrimination, the review provided in this section is admittedly less than exhaustive.

More recent surveys include Blau and Kahn (2017), which reviews the literature and provides new findings from an analysis of data from the Panel Study of Income Dynamics. Blau and Kahn conclude that by about 2010 only a small portion of the gender wage gap could be explained by human capital variables and that industry- and occupation-specific gender differences continued to be important. Lang and Lehmann (2011) also provide a comprehensive review of both theories of discrimination and associated empirical studies.

Perhaps by necessity, given the volume of literature that has emerged on the topic, other recent surveys have been more focused and narrower in their coverage. For example, Fang and Moro (2010) review models of statistical discrimination and affirmative action, while Jones (2008) surveys the literature on anti-discrimination policies and discrimination faced by workers with disabilities. Kunze (2008) and Charles and Guryan (2011) each review the empirical literature with an emphasis on the analytical methods used to examine labor market discrimination and the difficulties associated with various empirical techniques. Somewhat similarly, Weichselbaumer and Winter-Ebmer (2007) provide a meta-analysis of the literature and find, among other conclusions, that the choice of data to be examined can significantly affect a study's findings. Reflecting the increased use of experimental techniques to study labor market discrimination in recent years, Neumark (2018) offers a comprehensive survey that includes theoretical, empirical, and policy-related works. Finally, Kunze (2017) reviews the literature on gender wage gaps in developed countries and notes that, although women's labor force participation has increased in nearly all developed economies, a gender pay gap persists.

2.3.1 Economic Studies of Intersectional Wage Discrimination

At the outset, it is again worth noting that very few economic studies examine wage discrimination from an intersectional perspective. Ruwanpura (2008) considered the contributions of both mainstream and heterodox economists and, even though Akerlof and Kranton (2000) and Brewer et al. (2002) were identified as exceptions, concluded that "economists generally do not explicitly conceptualize multi-discrimination" (p. 87). The contributions of Akerlof and Kranton and of Brewer et al. may seem modest as neither explicitly examines intersectional wage discrimination. However, Akerlof and Kranton propose a model that suggests changing labor market patterns may be attributable to changes in social norms and gender associations, and Brewer et al. call for researchers to incorporate intersectionality when studying economic outcomes. In recent years, intersectional analysis has become more common in economic research. Even so, the topic of intersectional wage discrimination has generally remained the province of other disciplines.

At present, Kim (2009), Paul et al. (2022), and George et al. (2022) are the only economic studies of intersectional wage discrimination in the U.S. labor market. The latter two papers build on the work of Kim (2009), which examines CPS data for the year 2002 while focusing on wage discrimination against black women. The data sample is restricted to include wage and salary workers who range in age from 25 to 64 years and who earned at least $1 and worked at least one week during 2001. Students, members of the military, and the self-employed are excluded from the analysis; however, observations for which inferred hourly earnings fall below the corresponding state or federal minimum wage rate appear to have been retained. The final sample sizes ranged from 967 for black male workers to 7,295 for white males. As is common across studies of wage discrimination, the Blinder-Oaxaca decomposition technique is employed to estimate unexplained wage gaps; however, it appears that no adjustment is implemented to counter potential sample selection bias.

Kim estimates an ad hoc earnings function that is based on the traditional Mincer earnings model. Specifically, the dependent variable series is the natural logarithm of the hourly wage rate. Since hourly wage rates are inferred—i.e., calculated as annual earnings divided by the product of weeks worked and usual hours worked per week—both wage and salary employees are included in the analysis. The set of explanatory variables includes measures of educational attainment (i.e., high school diploma, college degree, and professional or graduate degree) and both age and age-squared—seemingly to proxy for potential labor force experience—to represent human capital attributes. However, the model also includes variables that indicate the number of children in the worker's household (0–6 and 6–17 years of age) and a series of dummy variables that identify (i) the region in which the worker resides, (ii) whether the worker is employed part-time (i.e., fewer than 34 hours worked in a usual week), (iii) if the worker lives in a central city, (iv) whether the worker is married, (v) the worker's union membership status or coverage under a collective bargaining agreement, (vi) if the worker has a disability that limits the types of work performed, and (vii) whether the worker is of Hispanic ethnicity. In separate regressions, Kim also includes sets of dummy variables to control for each worker's industry of employment, occupation classification, and whether they are employed in the public sector.

The dummy variable that represents Hispanic ethnicity is of particular interest. Owing to journal space limitations, Kim does not present a full complement of estimation results; however, it is noted that "People who worked part-time, were disabled, or Hispanic earned less" (p. 476). This suggests a statistically significant coefficient estimate for the dummy variable that identifies Hispanic ethnicity. George et al. (2022) correctly note that economic outcomes among Hispanic workers can be quite nuanced, varying according to national origin and imprecisely measured due to the complexity of ethnic self-identification among Hispanic individuals. Even so, Kim's finding of a statistically significant relationship between Hispanic ethnicity and hourly wages strongly suggests that the presence and/or extent of wage discrimination differs between Hispanic, black, female workers and non-Hispanic, black, female workers.

As part of Kim's analysis, black female workers were compared to black male workers and to white female workers, respectively, to determine the extent of any sex- or race-based wage discrimination.[7] The sum of any race- and sex-based discrimination was viewed as the expected discrimination rate. Black female workers were then compared to white male workers to identify an estimated discrimination rate. This approach is employed by Paul et al. (2022) and George et al. (2022), and it is used in the work presented here in Sect. 5.1.

Kim estimates that, in 2001, black male workers and black female workers earned less than their white male counterparts who possessed the same observable human capital. Specifically, black male workers were found to have earned 12% less than their white male counterparts while black female workers earned 27% less. For the black female workers, Kim estimates the extent of race- and sex-based discrimination as nine percent and 15%, respectively. Thus, the expected discrimination rate for black female workers is equal to 24%. The three percent difference between the expected and estimated discrimination rates is explained as additional

[7] Kim (2009), Paul et al. (2022), and George et al. (2022) use "penalty" and "penalties" when discussing unexplained wage gaps that may be attributed to wage discrimination. Consistent with our decision to risk overstatement rather than chance understatement of an important issue, "discrimination" is used here.

intersectional (i.e., simultaneous race- and sex-based) discrimination. Because the estimated discrimination rate differs from the expected rate (i.e., the sum of the sex- and race-based discrimination), Kim concludes that the wage discrimination suffered by black female workers is non-additive. This is consistent with Crenshaw's position that black female workers may face labor market discrimination that is unique and non-additive. It is important to note, however, that the intersectional wage discrimination reported by Kim became insignificant from zero once the author modified her empirical model to control for the industry of employment and occupation classification.

Paul et al. (2022) build on the work of Kim (2009) by addressing two related questions. First, the authors examine whether the magnitudes of wage discrimination, relative to a particular group, are the same for different groups. For example, relative to white male workers and white female workers, respectively, is race-based discrimination the same for black male workers and black female workers? Second, the authors revisit whether estimated wage discrimination values are additive or something other. While Paul et al. acknowledge other identities (e.g., nativity, country of origin, disability status, etc.) deserve attention, the focus of their study is restricted to race- and sex-based discrimination.

Paul et al. examine CPS data, focusing their primary analysis on 2017 but also examining data for 1980, 1990, 2005, and 2011. The sample examined includes full-time workers (i.e., 35 or more hours worked in the typical week) who range in age from 25 to 64 years and worked at least 26 weeks during the prior year. As in Kim (2009), members of the military and those who report being self-employed are excluded, and the dependent variable is the natural logarithm of the hourly wage rate.[8] The sample sizes vary from 2,903 black male workers to 18,681 white males. Also similar to Kim (2009), the authors employ the Blinder-Oaxaca decomposition technique but fail to account for potential sample selection bias even as they note "We exclude the unemployed and workers out of the labor force, which does introduce selection bias unless interpretation is extrapolated for only those in the labor market" (p. 24). The empirical model is very similar to the ad hoc specification employed by Kim (2009). The differences appear to be that Kim includes dummy variables to identify each worker's disabled status and union membership/coverage, while

[8] As is the case in Kim (2009), the authors do not explain how top-coded earnings values were treated.

Paul et al. do not. Additionally, Paul et al. include dummy variables in all estimations to represent each worker's industry of employment and occupation classification.

With respect to their first question, Paul et al. find variation in race- and sex-based discrimination across worker groups. For example, black male workers are estimated to face race-based discrimination equal to 11.3% while for black female workers the value is only 6.7%. Similarly, sex-based discrimination rates are found to vary across race classifications. Thus, the magnitudes of expected discrimination rates (i.e., the sums of personal characteristic-specific discrimination rates) are found to be conditional on the workers' unique combinations of identities. In response to their second question, Paul et al. find that their expected discrimination rates are not additive and that estimated discrimination rates that are associated with two or more identities are multiplicative or quantitatively nuanced. Additionally, contrary to the results reported by Kim, the authors find the additional intersectional discrimination that they observe for black female workers remains statistically significant even once industry of employment and occupation classification are controlled for and that the result persists across time.

In a departure from Kim (2009) and Paul et al. (2022), both of which examine CPS data, George et al. (2022) examine ACS data for the years 2010 and 2019 in addition to five percent samples of decennial census data from 1980, 1990, and 2000. Their sample composition is comparable to that examined by the two previous studies, including full-time (i.e., those employed 35 or more hours per week), non-farm, wage and salary workers, who are 25–64 years of age, and who report having worked 48 or more weeks in the prior year. Members of the military and those who are self-employed are excluded. Likewise, the authors exclude those who report annual earnings of $2 or less.

Consistent with Kim (2009) and Paul et al. (2022), George et al. employ the Blinder-Oaxaca estimation technique with an ad hoc Mincer-based earnings function. They also use the decomposition method of Chernozhukov et al. (2013) to decompose gaps at the 10th, 50th, and 90th percentiles of the wage distribution. While the authors do not employ any remedy for potential sample selection bias, unlike Kim (2009) and Paul et al. (2022), the authors do adjust top-coded values.

George et al. (2022) confirm and extend the findings of Kim (2009) and Paul et al. (2022). The authors examine Hispanic ethnicity, race, and sex, but Hispanic ethnicity is essentially treated as a separate race/ethnicity classification. More specifically, rather than categorizing female workers into four groups (i.e., non-Hispanic, black, females; non-Hispanic white, females; Hispanic, black, females; and Hispanic white, females), the authors opt for three categories: non-Hispanic, black, females; non-Hispanic white, females; and Hispanic females. This third group includes any Hispanic female worker regardless of whether their race classification is black or white.

Consistent with the earlier studies, the authors find the discrimination rate that is estimated for black women is greater than the sum of the estimated race- and sex-based discriminations (i.e., the expected discrimination rate). Thus, black female workers appear to suffer intersectional wage discrimination. This relationship persists throughout the study's reference period (i.e., 1980–2019). For Hispanic women, significant intersectional wage discrimination is found early in the reference period; however, in 2019, the estimated discrimination rate was approximately equal to the expected discrimination rate. George et al. (2022) also report that while white women have made progress in closing the wage gap during the past 40 years black and Hispanic women have made little or no progress.

2.4 Next Steps

In the next chapter, we describe our empirical methodology and present several examples that demonstrate the need for an analysis of intersectional wage discrimination in the U.S. labor market. In Chapters 4 and 5, we address several related questions. These questions include:

1. To what extent do we observe wage discrimination across worker groups that are defined by multiple intersecting identities (i.e., the personal characteristics of Hispanic ethnicity, nativity, race, and sex)?
2. Does observed wage discrimination vary across worker groups and, if so, does the variation follow a pattern(s) that suggests the discrimination is intersectional?
3. Is wage discrimination intersectional (i.e., is it additive or non-additive)?
4. Do we find evidence of a statistical relationship between pre-labor market wage discrimination with respect to the returns to schooling and intersectional wage discrimination?

Although at present there are only three economic studies of intersectional wage discrimination in the U.S. labor market, the existing works provide significant insights into the questions we seek to address. First, the studies present evidence that is consistent with the existence of intersectional wage discrimination. Second, the existing literature refutes the non-additive assumption and, thus, supports the argument that wage discrimination is frequently intersectional. Third, even though limited numbers of worker groups are considered in these earlier studies, each study provides some evidence of variation in estimated discrimination rates.

While the existing studies provide useful insights and guidance, the works are limited in terms of the personal characteristics considered and, thus, the number of worker groups considered. Additionally, to a lesser extent, whether due to limited data availability or simply as a matter of choice, the studies examine narrow time periods. We examine a lengthier period and larger data samples. We also consider more personal characteristics and, thus, many more intersecting identities (i.e., more worker groups). Examining our topic at finer levels of detail relative to earlier works allows for a considerable increase in our understanding of intersectionality and wage discrimination. Further, we extend the literature on intersectional discrimination by using our estimation results to examine potential pre-labor market discrimination related to schooling.

References

Aigner, Dennis J., and Glen G. Cain. 1977. Statistical Theories of Discrimination in Labor Markets. *Industrial and Labor Relations Review* 30: 175–187.

Akerlof, George A., and Rachel E. Kranton. 2000. Economics and Identity. *Quarterly Journal of Economics* 115 (3): 715–753.

Allport, Gordon. 1954. *The Nature of Prejudice*. New York: Doubleday Anchor Books.

Altonji, Joseph G., and Rebecca M. Blank. 1999. Race and Gender in the Labor Market. In *Handbook of Labor Economics*, ed. Orley Ashenfelter. Amsterdam: Elsevier.

Arrow, Kenneth J. 1972. Models of Job Discrimination. In *Racial Discrimination in Economic Life*, ed. A.H. Pascal, 83–102. Lexington, MA: D.C. Heath.

Arrow, Kenneth J. 1998. What Has Economics to Say About Racial Discrimination? *Journal of Economic Perspectives* 12 (2): 91–100.

Becker, Gary. 1957. *The Economics of Discrimination*. Chicago, IL: University of Chicago Press.

Blau, Francine D., and Lawrence M. Kahn. 2017. The Gender Wage Gap: Extent, Trends and Explanations. *Journal of Economic Literature* 55 (3): 789–865.

Brewer, Rose M., Cecilia A. Conrad, and Mary C. King. 2002. The Complexities and Potential of Theorizing Gender, Caste, Race, and Class. *Feminist Economics* 8 (2): 3–17.

Cain, Glen G. 1986. The Economic Analysis of Labor Market Discrimination: A Survey. In *Handbook of Labor Economics, Volume 1*, ed. Orley Ashenfelter and Richard Layard. Amsterdam: Elsevier.

Charles, Kerwin K., and Jonathan Guryan. 2011. Studying Discrimination: Fundamental Challenges and Recent Progress. *Annual Review of Economics* 3: 479–511.

Chernozhukov, Victor, Ivan Fernandez-Val, and Blaise Melly. 2013. Inference on Counterfactual Distributions. *Econometrica* 81 (6): 2205–2268.

D'Amico, Thomas F. 1987. The Conceit of Labor Market Discrimination. *The American Economic Review*: *Papers and Proceedings* 77 (2): 310–315.

Fang, Hanming, and Andrea Moro. 2010. Theories of Statistical Discrimination and Affirmative Action: A Survey. In *Handbook of Social Economics*, ed. Jess Benhabib, Alberto Bisin, and Matthew O. Jackson, vol. 1A: 134–200. Amsterdam: Elsevier.

Fiske, Susan T. 1998. Stereotyping, Prejudice, and Discrimination. In *Handbook of Social Psychology*, ed. Daniel Todd Gilbert, Susan T. Fiske, and Gardner Lindzey. New York: McGraw-Hill.

George, Erin E., Jessica Milli, and Sophie Tripp. 2022. Worse than a Double Whammy: The Intersectional Causes of Wage Inequality Between Women of Colour and White Men Over Time. *Labour* 36 (3): 302–341.

Hodson, Gordon, and Kristof Dhont. 2015. The Person-based Nature of Prejudice: Individual Difference Predictors of Intergroup Negativity. *European Review of Social Psychology* 26 (1): 1–42.

Jones, Melanie K. 2008. Disability and the Labour Market: A Review of the Empirical Evidence. *Journal of Economic Studies* 35 (5): 405–424.

Kim, Marlene. 2009. Race and Gender Differences in the Earnings of Black Workers. *Industrial Relations* 48 (3): 466–488.

Kirschenman, Joleen, and Kathryn M. Neckerman. 1991. We'd Love to Hire Them, But...": The Meaning of Race for Employers. In *The Urban Underclass*, ed. Christopher Jencks and Paul E. Peterson. Washington, DC: Brookings Institution Press.

Kruglanski, Arie W., Antonio Pierro, Lucia Mannetti, and Eraldo De Grada. 2006. Groups as Epistemic Providers: Need for Closure and the Unfolding of Group-centrism. *Psychological Review* 113 (1): 84–100.

Kunze, Astrid. 2008. Gender Wage Gap Studies: Consistency and Decomposition. *Empirical Economics* 35 (1): 63–76.
Kunze, Astrid. 2017. The Gender Wage Gap in Developed Countries. NHH Norwegian School of Economics.
Lang, Kevin, and Jee-Yeon K. Lehmann. 2011. Racial Discrimination in the Labor Market: Theory and Empirics. NBER Working Paper No. 17450.
Lundberg, Shelly J., and Richard Startz. 1983. Private Discrimination and Social Intervention in Competitive Labor Markets. *American Economic Review* 73 (3): 340–347.
Marshall, Ray. 1974. The Economics of Racial Discrimination: A Survey. *Journal of Economic Literature* 12 (3): 849–871.
Moss, Philip, and Chris Tilly. 2001. *Stories Employers Tell: Race, Skill and Hiring in America*. New York: Russell Sage Foundation.
Neumark, David. 2018. Experimental Research on Labor Market Discrimination. *Journal of Economic Literature* 56 (3): 799–866.
Paul, Mark, Khaing Zaw, and William Darity. 2022. Returns in the Labor Market: A Nuanced View of Penalties at the Intersection of Race and Gender. *Feminist Economics* 28 (2): 1–31.
Pettigrew, Thomas F., and Linda R. Tropp. 2006. A Meta-Analytic Test of Intergroup Contact Theory. *Journal of Personality and Social Psychology* 90 (5): 751–783.
Phelps, Edmund. 1972. The Statistical Theory of Racism and Sexism. *The American Economic Review* 62 (4): 659–661.
Quillian, Lincoln. 1995. Prejudice as a Response to Perceived Group Threat: Population Composition and Anti-immigrant and Racial Prejudice in Europe. *American Sociological Review* 60 (4): 586–611.
Ruwanpura, Kanchana N. 2008. Multiple Identities, Multiple Discrimination: A Critical Review. *Feminist Economics* 14 (3): 77–105.
Scheepers, Peer, Merove Gijsberts, and Marcel Coenders. 2002. Ethnic Exclusionism in European Countries Public Opposition to Civil Rights for Legal Migrants as a Response to Perceived Ethnic Threat. *European Sociological Review* 18 (1): 17–34.
Shulman, Steven. 1996. The Political Economy of Labor Market Discrimination: A Classroom-friendly Presentation of the Theory. *Review of Black Political Economy* 24 (4): 47–65.
Sidanius, Jim, Felicia Pratto, Colette van Laar, and Shana Levin. 2004. Social Dominance Theory: Its Agenda and Method. *Political Psychology* 25 (6): 845–880.
Stiglitz, Joseph E. 1973. Approaches to the Economics of Discrimination. *The American Economic Review* 63 (2): 287–295.
Varian, Hal R. 1992. What Use Is Economic Theory? Paper presented at the Is Economics Becoming a Hard Science? Conference, Paris, France.

Weichselbaumer, Doris, and Rudolph Winter-Ebmer. 2007. The Effects of Competition and Equal Treatment Laws on Gender Wage Differentials. *Economic Policy* 22: 235–287.

CHAPTER 3

Our Empirical Strategy: Mincer Earnings Functions and the Blinder-Oaxaca Technique

Abstract We provide a detailed introduction to the empirical methodology that we use to examine intersectional wage discrimination. First, we introduce and derive the Mincer earnings function and present our battery of corresponding regression models. We then illustrate the Mincer model by presenting estimation results that are obtained via regression analysis. Second, we introduce the Blinder-Oaxaca decomposition technique and the Heckman two-step selection bias correction procedure. This entails an initial discussion, an illustrative example, and a discussion of results obtained from several estimations.

Keyword American Community Survey (ACS) · Blinder-Oaxaca decomposition · Heckman two-step selection bias correction procedure · Mincer earnings function · Regression analysis

In Chapter 1, we introduced our topic, presented unadjusted wage gaps for several worker groups, and began to make a case for examining intersectional wage discrimination. In Chapter 2, we followed our overview of the dominant theories of discrimination with a review of the related economics literature. We now turn our attention to the empirical approach that we employ to examine intersectional wage discrimination. Since it serves as the cornerstone of our empirical strategy, we

R. White, *Intersectionality and Discrimination*,
https://doi.org/10.1007/978-3-031-26125-1_3

first introduce the Mincer earnings function, derive our primary estimation equation, and introduce three additional regression models that we include among our estimation equations. This is followed by discussions of the Blinder-Oaxaca decomposition technique and the Heckman sample selection model. Throughout this chapter, we further the case that multiple intersecting identities should be considered when examining wage discrimination. Toward this end and to foster a more complete understanding of our empirical approach, we close this chapter by extending our argument for the examination of intersectional wage discrimination by presenting results obtained from a series of preliminary estimations and subsequent decompositions.

3.1 The Mincer Earnings Function

Jacob Mincer (1958, 1974) was the first to derive an empirical model of wage earnings. In his model, earnings are presented as a function of education and labor market experience. During any period, a worker's observed earnings (i.e., their potential earnings less any human capital investment undertaken during the period) are depicted as a concave function of labor market experience.[1] Thus, assuming that an individual's formal schooling lasts S years and that any subsequent training (t) declines linearly over the lifecycle, the observed earnings (Y) of worker i are represented as a quadratic function of education and labor market experience. Equation (3.1) illustrates.

$$lnY_i(t) = \alpha_0 + \beta_1 S_i + \beta_2 t_i + \beta_3 t_i^2 + \varepsilon_{it} \tag{3.1}$$

Here, α_0 indicates the worker's initial earnings capacity (i.e., the worker's earnings conditional on their innate ability), β_1 is the rate of return to education, and β_2 and β_3 represent the return associated with on-the-job training. ε is an assumed stochastic error term.

Equation (3.1) is the Mincer earnings function. It may well be the most often used model in empirical research.[2] As a single-equation model,

[1] To be more precise, Mincer (1974) posited that wage setting at the time of hire was determined, at least in part, by workers' productive characteristics (e.g., schooling and experience).

[2] Rosen (1992) speaks to the widespread use of the Mincer earnings function: "It is virtually a 'rite of passage' for every young labor economist to have 'Mincered' some data or other" (p. 162).

it is elegant. It is also powerful as it allows for the identification of the relationships between human capital and workers' earnings. Human capital attributes (i.e., education and experience) may signal an employee's quality and other unobserved characteristics to a potential employer (Willis, 1986). Thus, it is not surprising that the Mincer equation is also referred to as the human capital earnings function.[3,4] In the remainder of this section, we detail the derivation of Eq. (3.1).

3.1.1 Derivation of the Mincer Equation

To begin, in Eq. (3.2), allow E_1 to represent a typical worker's earnings in period 1. Likewise, allow E_0 to represent the worker's potential earnings which, as noted, are based on the worker's innate abilities. Finally, allow C_0 to be the worker's effective dollar investment in human capital during period 0 (i.e., a measure of the skills carried into period 1), and let r represent the return to human capital investments made during the prior period.

$$E_1 = E_0 + rC_0 \tag{3.2}$$

The worker's earnings in the second period depend on the factors that determine their earnings in the initial period plus any returns from human capital investment that was undertaken during the initial period. Equation (3.3) illustrates this relationship over two periods.

$$E_2 = E_1 + rC_1 = E_0 + rC_0 + rC_1 \tag{3.3}$$

By recursion, we have Eq. (3.4), which indicates that a worker's earnings in any period t are the result of their innate ability and the cumulative human capital investments made in earlier periods.

$$E_t = E_0 + r\sum_{i=0}^{t-1} C_i \tag{3.4}$$

[3] Becker (2002) defines human capital as "the knowledge, information, ideas, skills, and health of individuals" (p. 3).

[4] Human capital theory assumes that workers enter the labor force with certain attributes/endowments that contribute to the individual's productivity and, thus, value to their employer (Becker 1994).

Because data on worker-specific dollar investments in human capital are not easily obtained, Mincer defined the share of earnings allocated to human capital investment in any period t as $k_t = \frac{C_t}{E_t}$. If we substitute for C_t in Eq. (3.4), take the natural logarithm of both sides of the resulting expression, acknowledge that $ln(1 + rk_i) \approx rk_i$ when rk_i is small, and make the corresponding substitution, we obtain Eq. (3.5).

$$lnE_t = lnE_0 + r\sum_{i=0}^{t-1} k_i \quad (3.5)$$

Further assuming that $k_i = 1$ when the typical worker is a student (i.e., that school is a full-time activity) and that k_i declines monotonically to reach 0 once the worker retires from the labor force, we can divide k_i into a full-time schooling period and a post-school investment period. The rate of return on human capital investment during the schooling period is given by r_s, and the rate of return during the post-schooling period is represented by r_p. The result is Eq. (3.6).

$$lnE_t = lnE_0 + r_sS + r_p\sum_{i=0}^{t-1} k_i \cong lnE_0 + r_sS + r_p\int_0^t k_j d_j \quad (3.6)$$

Although theory predicts k_j will decline monotonically, the rate of decline is simply not known. Most frequently, it is assumed that post-school investment declines linearly. Mincer assumed that k_0 represents the time-equivalent investment in the initial period with T representing the total number of periods during which investment occurs. Thus, substituting $k_t = k_0 + \frac{k_0}{T}T$ into Eq. (3.6) results in Eq. (3.7) which includes the familiar quadratic relationship between experience and potential earnings.

$$lnE_t = lnE_0 + r_sS + r_pk_ot - \frac{r_pk_o}{2T}t^2 \quad (3.7)$$

Because workers invest a portion of their earnings in human capital, observed earnings (Y) differ from potential earnings (E) such that observed earnings can be represented as $Y_t = (1 - k_t)E_t$. Taking the natural logarithm of both sides of this expression and substituting the result into Eq. (3.7), solving for actual earnings, and then substituting $k_0 + \frac{k_0}{T}T$ for k_t yields Eq. (3.8).

$$lnY_t = lnE_0 + r_s S + r_p k_o t - \frac{r_p k_o}{2T}t^2 + ln\left(1 - k_0 + \frac{k_0}{T}t\right) \tag{3.8}$$

Taking a two-term quadratic Taylor approximation of $ln\left(1 - k_0 + \frac{k_0}{T}t\right)$ yields Eq. (3.1), the Mincer earnings function that is presented at the beginning of this section. In the equation, $\alpha_o = lnE_0 - k_o\left(1 + \frac{k_0}{2}\right)$, $\beta_1 = r_s$, $\beta_2 = r_p k_o + \frac{k_0}{T}(1 + k_0)$, and $\beta_3 = -\frac{r_p k_o}{2T} - \frac{k_0^2}{2T^2}$.

Because differences in hourly wage rates may be attributable to the industry in which a worker is employed, their occupation, or their geographic location, when estimating our earnings functions we include fixed effects terms to identify each worker's industry of employment (Ω), their occupation classification (Ψ), and their state of residence (Θ).[5,6] The result is Eq. (3.9), the first of the four regression models that we estimate to discern the presence and extent of wage discrimination.

$$lnY_{it} = \alpha_0 + \beta_1 S_i + \beta_2 t_i + \beta_3 t_i^2 + \beta_\Omega \Omega_j + \beta_\Psi \Psi_k + \beta_\Theta \Theta_m + \varepsilon_i \tag{3.9}$$

Following Mincer, we alter Eq. (3.9) to allow for a quadratic relationship between education and earnings (Eq. 3.10). We also estimate a separate function (Eq. 3.11) that includes an interaction term between schooling and experience. This allows us to test whether earnings profiles are parallel across schooling levels. These are our second and third regression models.

$$\begin{aligned} lnY_i(t) = \alpha_0 &+ \beta_1 S_i + \beta_2 S_i^2 + \beta_3 t_i + \beta_4 t_i^2 + \beta_\Omega \Omega_j \\ &+ \beta_\Psi \Psi_k + \beta_\Theta \Theta_m + \varepsilon_i \end{aligned} \tag{3.10}$$

$$\begin{aligned} lnY_i(t) = \alpha_0 &+ \beta_1 S_i + \beta_2 S_i^2 + \beta_3 (S_i \times t_i) + \beta_4 t_i \\ &+ \beta_5 t_i^2 + \beta_\Omega \Omega_j + \beta_\Psi \Psi_k + \beta_\Theta \Theta_m + \varepsilon_i \end{aligned} \tag{3.11}$$

[5] Industry and occupation fixed effects are constructed using the ACS variables IND and OCC, respectively. Listings of industry and occupation classifications are provided in Appendix A.

[6] Further, because variation in wage rates may result from part-time or full-time employment status (Hirsch 2005; Blank 1990), we restrict our primary analysis to include only workers who are employed 32 or more hours in the typical week. We do, however, present estimates of wage discrimination for part-time workers. The results are discussed in Chapter 4.

Lastly, our fourth regression model is a slight variant of Eq. (3.9) in which the variable that represents years of education is replaced with a set of dummy variables that identify levels of educational attainment. Specifically, the categories identify whether the worker has (a) attained a high school diploma or its equivalent (HS), (b) completed some college coursework but has not earned a four-year degree (SC), (c) completed a bachelor's degree (BD), or (d) engaged in graduate study (GS) (i.e., has worked toward or completed a graduate degree). The null education classification in Eq. (3.12) is comprised of workers who lack a high school diploma.

$$
\begin{aligned}
lnY_i(t) = \alpha_0 + \beta_1 HS_i + \beta_2 SC_i + \beta_3 BD_i + \beta_4 GS_i + \beta_5 t_i + \beta_6 t_i^2 \\
+ \beta_\Omega \Omega_j + \beta_\Psi \Psi_k + \beta_\Theta \Theta_m + \varepsilon_i \qquad (3.12)
\end{aligned}
$$

3.1.2 *Illustrating the Mincer Equation*

To demonstrate our empirical process, we first estimate Eqs. (3.9) through (3.12) using ACS data for the year 2020. Descriptive statistics for the sample are presented in Table 3.1, and estimation results are provided in Table 3.2.

Table 3.1 Descriptive statistics, 2020 ACS data

Wage (dollars per hour)	32.5140
	(28.7693)
Education (years)	14.3860
	(2.9371)
Less than a High School Diploma	0.0516
	(0.2212)
High School Diploma	0.2142
	(0.4102)
Some College	0.2849
	(0.4514)
BA/BS Degree	0.2715
	(0.4447)
Graduate Study	0.1779
	(0.3824)
Experience (years)	23.7865
	(12.4967)

Note N = 742,489. Mean values presented with standard errors in parentheses

Table 3.2 Mincer earnings function results—all workers

Estimation equation	*(3.9)* *(a)*	*(3.10)* *(b)*	*(3.11)* *(c)*	*(3.12)* *(d)*
Education	0.0788***	−0.0433***	−0.0364***	
	(0.0003)	(0.0008)	(0.0012)	
Education x Education		0.0048***	0.0047***	
		(0.00003)	(0.00004)	
Education x Experience			−0.0001***	
			(0.00002)	
Experience	0.0313***	0.0338***	0.0362***	0.0344***
	(0.0002)	(0.0002)	(0.0004)	(0.0002)
Experience x Experience	−0.0004***	−0.0005***	−0.0005***	−0.0005***
	(4.1E-06)	(3.70E-06)	(4.0E-06)	(3.7E-06)
High School Diploma				0.1138***
				(0.0026)
Some College				0.2217***
				(0.0026)
BA/BS Degree				0.5445***
				(0.0028)
Graduate Study				0.7987***
				(0.0032)
Constant	1.8027***	2.5232***	2.4461***	2.5556***
	(0.0123)	(0.0127)	(0.0162)	(0.0118)
N	742,489	742,489	742,489	742,489
F statistic	4,232.20***	4,896.88***	4,969.67***	4,896.41
R-squared	0.3746	0.3969	0.3970	0.3964

Note Robust standard errors in parentheses. All estimations include industry, occupation, and state of residence fixed effects. "***", "**", and "*" denote statistical significance from zero at the 1%, 5%, and 10% levels, respectively

We see that, in 2020, the typical worker in our sample earned an hourly wage equal to $32.51.[7,8] We also see that the educational attainment of the typical worker was slightly less than 14.4 years. Looking at the education classifications, we see that slightly more than one-quarter of the workers in our sample either failed to complete high school (5.2%) or earned a high school diploma or equivalent degree (i.e., a GED) but completed no additional education (21.4%). Similar proportions of workers completed some college coursework but failed to complete a four-year degree (28.5%) or attained a four-year degree but did not pursue graduate study (27.2%). About one in six workers in the data set (17.8%) completed at least some coursework toward a graduate degree. Additionally, the labor market experience of the typical worker was nearly 23.8 years.[9] Due to the limitations of the ACS data, we can only measure potential labor market experience. Specifically, the experience variable is constructed as the worker's age minus their years of education minus six.[10]

Turning attention to Table 3.2, the results obtained from the estimation of Eq. (3.9) are presented in column (a). We see the anticipated positive relationship between education and observed earnings. All else held constant, an additional year of education is estimated to increase the hourly wage of the typical worker by 7.88%. Additionally, given the positive coefficient estimate for the experience variable and the negative coefficient for the experience-squared variable, we also find, again holding all else constant, that earnings increase, as expected, at a

[7] The wage series imputes the hourly wage rate by dividing each worker's reported wage or salary income during the past 12 months by the product of the number of weeks worked during the past 12 months and their usual hours worked per week during the past 12 months. Thus, the series includes the hourly earnings of both wage and salary workers.

[8] Observations for which the value of the wage variable is less than the minimum wage rate in the corresponding worker's state of residence are removed from the data set.

[9] The pairwise correlation coefficients for the hourly wage series and the educational attainment (in years) and experience variables are 0.3305 and 0.0681, respectively.

[10] While it is not uncommon for researchers to construct the measure of potential labor market experience as age minus years of education minus five, we follow the construction employed by Dell'Aringa et al. (2015), Fadlon (2015), Jolly (2012), and many others. For example, the experience variable takes a value of zero for an 18-year-old worker who has completed 12 years of schooling (i.e., potential experience = 18 − 12 − 6 = 0).

slightly decreasing rate with more years of experience (i.e., a non-linear relationship between experience and hourly earnings).

The estimation of Eq. (3.12) produces coefficient estimates for the experience variables that are similar to those obtained from the estimation of Eq. (3.9). This is to be expected since the only difference between the two estimations is how educational attainment is represented. In Eq. (3.9), education is measured in years of schooling completed, while in Eq. (3.12) education is measured by the level of attainment. We see that all else equal, workers who complete a high school diploma or an equivalent credential earn 11.38% more per hour than an otherwise comparable worker who has less than a high school education. Similarly, workers who complete some college coursework earn 22.17% more than a worker who has not completed high school. Additionally, workers who complete a four-year college degree and those who undertake graduate study earn 54.45% and 79.87% more per hour, respectively, than a worker who lacks a high school education.

Finally, the remaining two regression models, for which results are presented in columns (b) and (c), allow for a quadratic effect of education on earnings (Eq. 3.10) and both a quadratic earnings effect and an interaction effect between education and earnings (Eq. 3.11). We see an exponential relationship between education and earnings, and the coefficient estimate for the education-experience interaction term, while statistically significant, is so low as to be of minimal practical significance. Thus, it appears that earnings profiles are in fact parallel (or nearly parallel) across schooling levels when educational attainment is measured in years of schooling completed.

The description and derivation of the Mincer equation that is offered in this section and the results that are presented in Table 3.2 provide a primary understanding of our empirical strategy. Identifying the portions of the differences in mean hourly wage rates across worker groups that are attributable to differences in productive characteristics and the portion which remains unexplained and, thus, can be attributed to wage discrimination requires a slightly more complex approach. If we simply modify Eq. (3.9) such that a set of dummy variables represents the categorization of workers into groups based on their multiple intersecting identities, the resulting estimation equation would suffer from the assumption that the returns to education and experience are equivalent across worker groups. We examine variation in the returns to education in Chapter 5;

however, at this point, we can simply note that the returns to schooling vary considerably across worker groups.

To properly address the topic of wage discrimination, we adopt the standard approach employed by observational studies in the literature. As is previously noted, this involves the use of the Blinder-Oaxaca decomposition technique (Blinder 1973; Oaxaca 1973) while correcting for potential self-selection bias using the two-step methodology proposed by Heckman (1979).[11] The remainder of this chapter details our estimation technique and strategy while providing several examples that further illustrate the need for an analysis of intersectional wage discrimination.

3.2 The Blinder-Oaxaca Decomposition Technique

As noted in our initial chapter, differences in mean hourly wage rates (i.e., the unadjusted wage gap) are often presented as evidence of wage discrimination. Comparing the average hourly wage rate of female workers to that of their male counterparts and concluding that the difference is indicative of sex-based wage discrimination is problematic since such an approach is unlikely to compare equally skilled men and women. Some portion of the wage gap may be attributable to the fact that, on average, women have different levels of ability, schooling, experience, or training relative to the typical male worker. Similarly, it may be that women and men self-select into different occupations or seek employment in different industries which may also contribute to variation in hourly wage rates. An alternative approach to estimating sex-based wage discrimination that yields more accurate results involves the comparison of wages for equally skilled female and male workers. Identifying the difference in the wages of women and men who have the same levels of education and experience and who are employed in the same occupation and industry provides a much better indication of how much of the unadjusted wage differential may be attributed to discrimination.

[11] Cotton (1988), Neumark (1988), and Oaxaca and Ransom (1994) each offer refinements of the Blinder-Oaxaca decomposition technique. See Bauer and Sinning (2008) and Yun (2004) for extensions of the Blinder-Oaxaca technique to non-linear models. Additionally, Bauer and Sinning (2010) and Fairlie (2005) extend the technique to logit, probit, and tobit models.

3.2.1 *Illustrating the Blinder-Oaxaca Technique*

The Blinder-Oaxaca decomposition technique takes the unadjusted wage gap and divides it into two portions, one that is related to differences in productive characteristics and another that can be attributed to labor market discrimination.[12,13] Fig. 3.1 helps to illustrate the technique. Here, the figure depicts earnings functions for black workers and white workers, with the earnings functions assumed to differ across the two worker groups.[14] To simplify, assume that education is the only determinant of productivity and, thus, the only determinant of the hourly wage rate. The wage gap that can be attributed to a difference in schooling is then the difference in the skill portion. Any remaining wage difference can be attributed to potential discrimination.

Assume that the data show the average white worker has more schooling than the average black worker, with $\overline{\overline{S}}_b$ and $\overline{\overline{S}}_w$ representing the average years of schooling for black and white workers, respectively. Given the simplifying assumption that schooling is the only determinant of the hourly wage rate, we should expect to see a higher average hourly wage rate for white workers as compared to black workers. In this scenario, we can see that at least some portion of the unadjusted wage gap is due to differences in levels of education/productivity and, thus, is not the result of discrimination.

Given the assumed levels of education and the relationship between years of schooling and hourly wage rates, we can first identify the unadjusted wage gap. Since the average white worker has $\overline{\overline{S}}_w$ years of schooling, the corresponding average hourly wage rate will equal $\overline{\overline{W}}_w$. Similarly, the average hourly wage rate of black workers, given $\overline{\overline{S}}_b$ years of schooling, will equal $\overline{\overline{W}}_b$. The unadjusted wage differential is then $\overline{\overline{W}}_w - \overline{\overline{W}}_b$.

[12] Fortin et al. (2010) provide an excellent survey of decomposition methods in economics, including the Blinder-Oaxaca technique.

[13] It is important to again note that for the entire unexplained portion of the log difference in predicted hourly wage rates to be attributable to discrimination, all determinants of the hourly wage rate must be accounted for by the regression model. Otherwise, discrimination may be overstated or understated.

[14] For simplicity, we are only considering the workers' racial identities and are limiting the example to black workers and white workers.

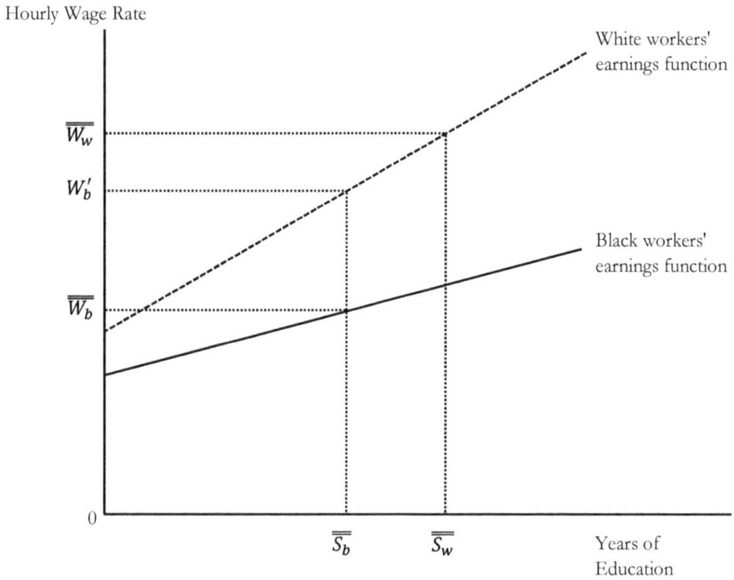

Fig. 3.1 Illustration of Blinder-Oaxaca decomposition technique I

Perhaps the most straightforward way to decompose the unadjusted wage gap to account for group differences in productive characteristics is to think about the average black worker. This representative worker has $\overline{\overline{S}}_b$ years of education, and in Fig. 3.1, their hourly wage rate is determined by the solid line. This shows how education translates into earnings for black workers. The dashed line illustrates the earnings function for white workers, so if the black worker was instead white their wages would be determined by the dashed line. In such an instance, given their $\overline{\overline{S}}_b$ years of schooling, the worker would earn a wage equal to W_b'. This reveals wage discrimination. That is, given the workers' productive characteristics, the difference between what the worker would earn if they were white and what they do earn being black (i.e., $W_b' - \overline{\overline{W}}_b$) represents wage discrimination. The rest of the difference in wages (i.e., $\overline{\overline{W}}_w - W_b'$) is because, on average in this example, white workers complete a different level of schooling.

To fill out this example somewhat, we can assume that we estimate separate wage regressions for the two worker groups and that the results for the hourly earnings of the black worker group and the white worker group are given, respectively, by Eqs. (3.13) and (3.14).[15]

$$W_b = 9.1 + 0.14S \tag{3.13}$$

$$W_w = 10.7 + 0.25S \tag{3.14}$$

If we further assume that black workers have, on average, 13 years of schooling while white workers have, again on average, 15 years of schooling, we can determine the unadjusted wage gap.

$$\overline{\overline{W}}_b = 9.1 + 0.14 \times 13 = 9.1 + 1.82 = 10.92$$

$$\overline{\overline{W}}_w = 10.7 + 0.25 \times 15 = 10.7 + 3.75 = 14.45$$

$$\overline{\overline{W}}_w - \overline{\overline{W}}_b = 14.45 - 10.92 = 3.53$$

Here, on average, black workers are paid \$3.53 less per hour than white workers (i.e., a difference of 24.43%).

In our example, the average white worker has more years of schooling relative to the average black worker. The difference in schooling, which is assumed to translate to a difference in productivity, explains a portion of the \$3.53 unadjusted wage gap. To identify how much of the unadjusted wage gap is due to the difference in schooling and how much is attributable to discrimination, we can calculate the expected wage of the average black worker if they were white. To do this, we take the average black worker's 13 years of schooling and substitute that into the white workers' wage equation (i.e., Eq. 3.14).

$$W_b^{'} = 10.7 + 0.25 \times 13 = 10.7 + 3.25 = 13.95$$

[15] Note that the coefficient values vary across the earnings functions. This would reflect a lower rate of return to schooling for black workers as compared to white workers and can be explained as possible pre-labor market discrimination. As has been noted, we focus on differences in returns to education in Chapter 5.

We then compare this value to what the average black worker actually earns to identify the adjusted wage gap.

$$W_b' - \overline{\overline{W}}_b = 13.95 - 10.92 = 3.03$$

The Blinder-Oaxaca decomposition allows the unadjusted wage gap to be adjusted to account for differences in productive characteristics. The residual unexplained gap, thus, is indicative of the combined influences of all non-market characteristics. Thus, the adjusted wage gap reveals that \$3.03 of the \$3.53 wage gap may be attributable to differences in race (i.e., discrimination). Stated differently, 14.16% of the unadjusted wage gap (i.e., $\overline{\overline{W}}_w - \overline{\overline{W}}_b = \$14.45 - \$13.95 = \$0.50$) is explained by differences in schooling. The remaining 85.84% of the unadjusted gap (i.e., $W_b' - \overline{\overline{W}}_b = \$3.03$) remains unexplained and, thus, is potentially attributable to discrimination. See Fig. 3.2 for an illustration.

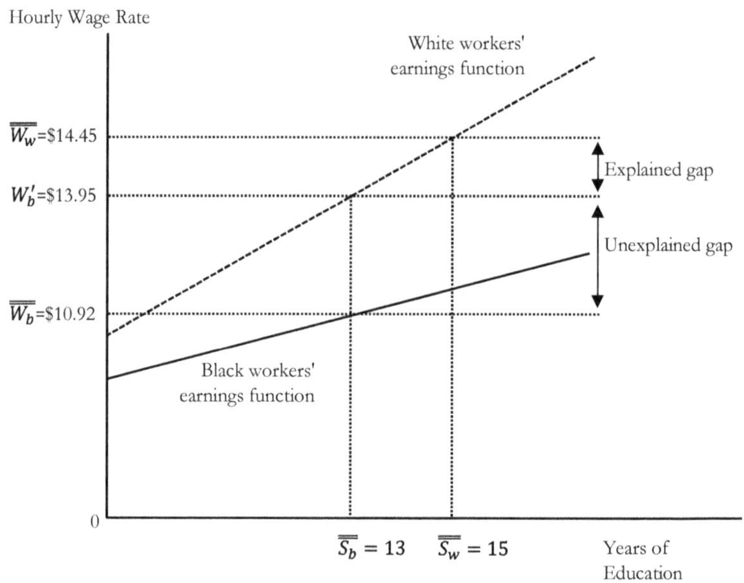

Fig. 3.2 Illustration of Blinder-Oaxaca decomposition technique II

As noted at the beginning of this chapter, when we apply the Blinder-Oaxaca decomposition technique to our data, we do so in conjunction with the Heckman two-step selection bias correction procedure (Heckman 1976, 1979).[16] With respect to our examination of the wage gap, sample selection may be an issue if the observations that are evaluated by our estimations are not representative of the working-age population. If we are examining a random sample of workers, estimation of our models and obtaining coefficient estimates are straightforward. However, it may be that we only observe hourly wage rates, our dependent variable series, if the observations in the random sample first make some decisions. A pertinent decision would be to choose to enter the labor force and seek employment. If the result of those decisions produces a distorted representation of the working-age population, then coefficients estimated without correction for the sample selection may be biased (Heckman 1990).

We model the decision to enter the labor force (LF) as a function of an individual i's years of educational attainment (S), their age (Age and Age^2), whether they are married ($Married$) or widowed, divorced, or separated (Wid_div_sep), whether individual i is a homeowner (Own), and variables related to the individual's household j that include whether English is commonly spoken in the household (Eng), the number of children ages 0 through 6 years in the household ($Kids0\_6$), and the number of children ages 7 through 17 years in the household ($Kids7\_17$). Specifically, Eq. (3.15) illustrates our selection model.

$$\begin{aligned} LF_i = {} & \alpha_0 + \beta_1 S_i + \beta_2 Age_i + \beta_3 Age_i^2 + \beta_4 Married_i \\ & + \beta_5 Wid\_div\_sep_i + \beta_6 Own_i + \beta_7 Eng_j \\ & + \beta_8 Kids0\_6_j + \beta_9 Kids7\_17_j \end{aligned} \tag{3.15}$$

[16] The first step involves the estimation of a probit model where labor force participation is the dependent variable. From the fitted model, the inverse Mills ratio is then estimated for each observation in the available data. The second step is the estimation of the wage equation for the sub-sample while including the inverse Mills ratio as an explanatory variable.

3.2.2 *The Decomposition Technique in Practice*

To demonstrate the Blinder-Oaxaca decomposition technique and, by doing so, further impress the need for an analysis of intersectional discrimination, we now apply the technique to examine the wage gaps between several broad groups of workers. We examine data from the 2020 ACS by first estimating slight variants of Eqs. (3.9) and (3.12) to compare black workers to white workers.[17,18] We then estimate these same equations to evaluate the wage gaps between female workers and male workers. This is followed by the estimation of our variants of Eqs. (3.9) and (3.12) to compare three additional worker groups—white female workers, black female workers, and black male workers—to the null cohort that includes white male workers.

We begin by reviewing the descriptive statistics presented in Table 3.3, placing particular focus on the mean hourly wage rates. We see that, on average, white workers earn an hourly wage rate of $33.38. This is $7.70 higher than the average hourly wage rate of black workers—resulting in a 23.05% unadjusted wage gap. We also see that male workers earn, again on average, $6.65 more than their female counterparts—an unadjusted gap of 18.74%. Finally, comparing the average hourly wage rate of white male workers ($36.79) to the remaining three worker groups, we find unadjusted wage gaps of 20.92% for white females, 28.36% for black males, and 31.78% for black females.

Turning attention to the variables that represent productive characteristics, white workers possess, on average, 14.57 years of education while black workers have completed, on average, 13.91 years of schooling. Female workers have a high average level of education (14.75 years) relative to male workers (14.09 years); thus, white female workers have a higher average education level (14.92 years) than do white male workers (14.29 years), black female workers (14.26 years), and black male workers (13.5 years).

White workers and black workers have quite similar average levels of potential labor force experience (i.e., a difference of fewer than 0.5 years).

[17] See Jann (2008) for a detailed discussion of the Blinder-Oaxaca technique and its implementation in Stata.

[18] The deviations from Eqs. (3.9) and (3.12) involve the inclusion of two dummy variables, one to identify whether workers are foreign-born and another to identify whether workers are Hispanic.

Table 3.3 Descriptive statistics—select worker groups

Cohort n	*Black* *60,189* *(a)*	*White* *524,192* *(b)*	*Female* *333,189* *(c)*	*Male* *409,300* *(d)*	*Black Female* *31,896* *(e)*	*Black Male* *28,293* *(f)*	*White Female* *231,948* *(g)*	*White Male* *292,244* *(h)*
Hourly wage rate	25.6859 (20.7945)	33.3813 (29.3557)	28.8462 (23.3337)	35.4998 (32.2236)	25.0937 (19.5432)	26.3536 (22.1018)	29.0919 (23.1123)	36.7857 (33.0993)
Education (in years)	13.9057 (2.7385)	14.5697 (2.6629)	14.7539 (2.7930)	14.0865 (3.0164)	14.2643 (2.7438)	13.5013 (2.6756)	14.9182 (2.5741)	14.2932 (2.6996)
Less than H.S. diploma	0.0563 (0.2305)	0.0328 (0.1781)	0.0338 (0.1807)	0.0661 (0.2484)	0.0430 (0.2028)	0.0713 (0.2574)	0.0200 (0.1400)	0.0430 (0.2028)
High school diploma	0.2615 (0.4394)	0.2119 (0.4087)	0.1707 (0.3763)	0.2495 (0.4327)	0.2073 (0.4054)	0.3226 (0.4675)	0.1664 (0.3724)	0.2481 (0.4319)
Some college completed	0.3421 (0.4744)	0.2889 (0.4533)	0.2920 (0.4547)	0.2791 (0.4486)	0.3537 (0.4781)	0.3291 (0.4699)	0.2914 (0.4544)	0.2869 (0.4523)
B.A./B.S. degree	0.2011 (0.4008)	0.2861 (0.4519)	0.2944 (0.4558)	0.2529 (0.4347)	0.2223 (0.4158)	0.1772 (0.3818)	0.3069 (0.4612)	0.2696 (0.4437)
Graduate study	0.1390 (0.3460)	0.1802 (0.3844)	0.2091 (0.4067)	0.1525 (0.3595)	0.1737 (0.3789)	0.0999 (0.2998)	0.2152 (0.4110)	0.1525 (0.3595)
Experience (in years)	24.6208 (12.1911)	24.1372 (12.5268)	23.5855 (12.5841)	23.9502 (12.4226)	24.6058 (12.1410)	24.6377 (12.2475)	23.9414 (12.6701)	24.2925 (12.4097)
Homeowner	0.5533 (0.4972)	0.7838 (0.4117)	0.7379 (0.4398)	0.7387 (0.4394)	0.5520 (0.4973)	0.5547 (0.4970)	0.7826 (0.4125)	0.7847 (0.4110)

(continued)

Table 3.3 (continued)

Cohort	*Black*	*White*	*Female*	*Male*	*Black Female*	*Black Male*	*White Female*	*White Male*
n	*60,189*	*524,192*	*333,189*	*409,300*	*31,896*	*28,293*	*231,948*	*292,244*
	(a)	*(b)*	*(c)*	*(d)*	*(e)*	*(f)*	*(g)*	*(h)*
Kids 0–6 years of age in Household	0.1583	0.1602	0.1553	0.1788	0.1636	0.1522	0.1452	0.1722
	(0.365)	(0.3668)	(0.3622)	(0.3832)	(0.3699)	(0.3592)	(0.3523)	(0.3776)
Kids 7–17 years of age in Household	0.3144	0.2923	0.3044	0.3142	0.3396	0.2861	0.2825	0.3000
	(0.4643)	(0.4548)	(0.4601)	(0.4642)	(0.4736)	(0.4520)	(0.4502)	(0.4583)
English-speaking Household	0.9030	0.9382	0.8433	0.8364	0.9124	0.8923	0.9395	0.9372
	(0.2960)	(0.2408)	(0.3635)	(0.3699)	(0.2827)	(0.3100)	(0.2384)	(0.2427)
Age	43.5265	43.7069	43.3394	43.0367	43.8701	43.1390	43.8596	43.5857
	(11.8979)	(12.1421)	(12.0367)	(12.0494)	(11.8131)	(11.9811)	(12.1459)	(12.1378)
Married	0.4070	0.6286	0.5699	0.6239	0.3552	0.4654	0.6054	0.6470
	(0.4913)	(0.4832)	(0.4951)	(0.4844)	(0.4786)	(0.4988)	(0.4888)	(0.4779)
Single	0.4087	0.2364	0.2594	0.2701	0.4247	0.3907	0.2257	0.2449
	(0.4916)	(0.4249)	(0.4383)	(0.4440)	(0.4943)	(0.4879)	(0.4180)	(0.4300)
Widowed, Divorced, or Separated	0.1843	0.1351	0.1707	0.1061	0.2201	0.1439	0.1690	0.1082
	(0.3877)	(0.3418)	(0.3763)	(0.3079)	(0.4143)	(0.3509)	(0.3747)	(0.3106)

Note Mean values presented with standard deviations in parentheses

Male and female workers also have similar average values for years of potential experience; thus, it is unsurprising that white male workers (24.29 years, on average) do not differ considerably from black female workers (24.61 years), black male workers (24.64 years), and white female workers (23.94 years) in this regard. While comparisons of average years of education across worker groups are telling, additional details are found when comparing the proportions of worker groups in each of the educational attainment categories. From columns (a) through (d), we see that, relative to white workers, black workers are more likely to not have earned a college degree. We also see that female workers, regardless of race, are more likely than their male counterparts to either complete some college or earn a college degree. Looking at columns (e) through (h), we see that nearly 40% of black male workers have earned, at most, a high school diploma while, by comparison, more than half (52.21%) of white female workers have earned a college degree.

The bottom half of Table 3.3 presents the descriptive statistics for the variables that are used in our sample selection estimations. We see that, while the female and male worker groups have similar mean values for most variables, stark differences are found when comparing black and white worker groups. Namely, white workers are more than 40% more likely to own a home as compared to black workers. Additionally, white workers are more likely to be married and less likely to be single or to be widowed, divorced, or separated relative to black workers. Similar differences are found when comparing the white male, white female, black male, and black female worker groups.

Given the differences in average hourly wage rates and average values for education and, to lesser extents, potential labor force experience across worker groups, estimating the extent of potential wage discrimination requires the application of the Blinder-Oaxaca technique. The first set of results—obtained when comparing black workers to white workers—is presented in Table 3.4[19]. The results presented in columns (a) and (b) correspond to the estimation of Eq. (3.9), while the results presented in columns (c) and (d) correspond to the estimation of Eq. (3.12).

Across both sets of results, we see that the returns to investment in human capital are higher for white workers yet still generally positive and statistically significant from zero for black workers. Similarly, we see higher

[19] Results obtained from the estimation of the corresponding Heckman sample selection model are presented in Appendix B.

Table 3.4 Estimation results—black workers relative to white workers

Group	*Black*	*White*	*Black*	*White*
Estimation equation	*(3.9)*	*(3.9)*	*(3.12)*	*(3.12)*
	(a)	*(b)*	*(c)*	*(d)*
Education	0.0530***	0.0896***		
	(0.0013)	(0.0003)		
High School graduate			−0.0136	0.0979***
			(0.0167)	(0.0039)
Some college			0.0515***	0.2014***
			(0.0171)	(0.0039)
B.A./B.S			0.2778***	0.5342***
			(0.0194)	(0.0040)
Graduate study			0.4797***	0.7811***
			(0.0212)	(0.0043)
Experience	0.0120***	0.0351***	0.0209***	0.0368***
	(0.0010)	(0.0002)	(0.0014)	(0.0002)
Experience squared	−0.0002***	−0.0005***	−0.0003***	−0.0006***
	(1.9e-05)	(4.7e-06)	(2.6e-05)	(4.6e-06)
Constant	2.0719***	1.6494***	2.6629***	2.5690***
	(0.1742)	(0.0190)	(0.2404)	(0.0187)
N	60,189	524,192	60,189	524,192
Selected	58,142		58,142	
Non-selected	2,047		2,047	
Adjusted R-squared		0.3815		0.3933
F statistic		3.440.33***		3,503.80***
Wald Statistic	11,359.80***		6,617.00***	

Note See Table 3.2 notes

returns to potential labor market experience for white workers relative to black workers. The former finding may indicate pre-market discrimination that allows white workers to gain higher quality education relative to black workers. The latter may reflect greater opportunities for promotion to higher-paying positions for white workers relative to their black counterparts. For both worker groups and in both estimations, we see that earnings increase with experience at slightly decreasing rates.

The differences in predicted log hourly wage rates are presented in Table 3.5. Here, the values presented in column (a) correspond to the results presented in columns (a) and (b) of Table 3.4, and the values presented in column (b) of Table 3.5 map to the results provided in columns (c) and (d) of Table 3.4. Looking first at column (a), we see the log difference is equal to 16.87%. The decomposition of this difference reveals that nearly half (i.e., 8.4%) of the unadjusted wage gap is attributable to differences in worker endowments (i.e., the explanatory variables in the regression model). A negligible 0.24% is attributable to differences in coefficients and endowments that exist simultaneously between the two worker groups. The remaining portion of the difference is the wage discrimination component of the unadjusted wage gap. It is interpreted as the typical black worker receiving an hourly wage that is 8.23% less than the rate received by a comparable (i.e., equally skilled) white worker. Similar results are presented in column (b). The unadjusted difference is equal to 15.08%. This difference is decomposed into the endowment effect (8.39%), an interaction effect (0.27%), and the residual difference that can be attributed to wage discrimination (6.42%).

In Tables 3.4 and 3.5, we document the unexplained portions of the wage gap between black workers and white workers. These values may serve as approximations of the wage discrimination faced by black workers. The corresponding estimations only allow for differences in race (i.e., black or white) and do not consider other worker identities on which disparate treatment may be based. To add another layer to the analysis and, in doing so, demonstrate the need for an analysis of intersectional wage discrimination, we again estimate our variants of Eqs. (3.9) and (3.12); however, we now compare race-sex pairings to a null cohort of white male workers. Specifically, we consider black males, black females, and white females, separately, in relation to white male workers to identify the unexplained portions of the wage gaps (i.e., our estimates of wage discrimination).

Table 3.5 Blinder-Oaxaca decompositions—black workers relative to white workers

Estimation equation	*(3.9)* *(a)*	*(3.12)* *(b)*
Differential		
Predicted Log Wage Rate: Black	3.1246***	3.1425***
	(0.0055)	(0.0072)
Predicted Log Wage Rate: White	3.2933***	3.2933***
	(0.0008)	(0.0008)
Unadjusted Difference	0.1687***	0.1508***
	(0.0056)	(0.0072)
Decomposition of Unadjusted Difference		
Portion Attributable to Endowments	0.0840***	0.0839***
	(0.0035)	(0.0047)
Portion Attributable to Coefficients	0.0823***	0.0642***
	(0.0055)	(0.0072)
Interaction (Simultaneously Attributed to Endowments and Coefficients)	0.0024	0.0027
	(0.0034)	(0.0046)

Note Differentials and decompositions correspond to results presented in Table 3.4

In Table 3.6, results that correspond to the estimation of Eq. (3.9) are presented in columns (a) through (d). The values in column (d) apply to the white male worker group and, thus, do not change across the three estimations that compare white males to black female workers (results provided in column [a]), black male workers (column [b]), and white female workers (column [c]). As in Table 3.4, we see variation in the returns to education and in the returns to experience across worker groups, with returns being greater for white workers than for black workers. Similar patterns of relative magnitudes are found in columns (e) through (h) where the results obtained from the estimation of Eq. (3.12) are presented. Looking at the coefficients of the experience and experience-squared variables, we see that the related returns of white male workers are (i) considerably higher than the returns of white female workers, (ii) nearly twice the level of returns for black male workers, and (iii) more than twice the returns realized by black female workers. This is found for both estimations.

Based on the results in Table 3.6, for both estimation equations, log differences between white male workers and the three remaining worker groups are presented in Table 3.7. The unexplained portions of the

Table 3.6 Estimation results—black female, black male, and white female workers relative to white male workers

Group Estimation equation	*Black female (3.9) (a)*	*Black male (3.9) (b)*	*White female (3.9) (c)*	*White male (3.9) (d)*	*Black female (3.12) (e)*	*Black male (3.12) (f)*	*White female (3.12) (g)*	*White male (3.12) (h)*
Education (in years)	0.0601***	0.0458***	0.0907***	0.0863***				
	(0.0032)	(0.0016)	(0.0006)	(0.0004)				
High school diploma					−0.0137	−0.0031	0.0729***	0.1183***
					(0.0445)	(0.0157)	(0.0068)	(0.0048)
Some college completed					0.0535	0.0713***	0.1837***	0.2375***
					(0.0453)	(0.0163)	(0.0068)	(0.0048)
B.A./B.S. degree					0.2904***	0.2816***	0.4971***	0.5570***
					(0.0515)	(0.0189)	(0.0069)	(0.0050)
Graduate study					0.4984***	0.4819***	0.7367***	0.8018***
					(0.0556)	(0.0214)	(0.0071)	(0.0054)
Experience	0.0175***	0.0220***	0.0257***	0.0399***	0.0181***	0.0233***	0.0285***	0.0415***
	(0.0026)	(0.0012)	(0.0007)	(0.0003)	(0.0039)	(0.0014)	(0.0005)	(0.0003)
Experience squared	– 0.0002***	– 0.0003***	−0.0004***	0.0006	– 0.0002***	– 0.0003***	−0.0004***	– 0.0006***
	(0.00005)	(0.00002)	(0.00002)	(6.5e-06)	(0.0001)	(0.00003)	(0.00001)	(6.4e-06)
Constant	1.9234***	2.2035***	1.7235***	1.7213***	2.9112***	2.6812***	−0.0292	2.5767***
	(0.4153)	(0.2116)	(0.0372)	(0.0217)	(1.0050)	(0.2461)	(0.0954)	(0.0211)
N	31,896	28,293	231,948	294,244	31,896	28,293	231,948	294,244

(continued)

Table 3.6 (continued)

Group	*Black female*	*Black male*	*White female*	*White male*	*Black female*	*Black male*	*White female*	*White male*
Estimation equation	*(3.9)* *(a)*	*(3.9)* *(b)*	*(3.9)* *(c)*	*(3.9)* *(d)*	*(3.12)* *(e)*	*(3.12)* *(f)*	*(3.12)* *(g)*	*(3.12)* *(h)*
Selected	31,192	26,950	228,286		31,192	26,950	228,286	
Non-selected	704	1,343	3,662		704	1,343	3,662	
Adjusted R-squared				0.3915				0.4032
F statistic				2,000.89***				2,036.28***
Wald statistic	2,536.62***	7,420.25***	69,527.27***		1,228.00***	5,995.26***	139,310.40***	

Note See Table 3.2 notes

Table 3.7 Blinder-Oaxaca decompositions—black female, black male, and white female workers relative to white male workers

Group	*Black male*		*Black female*		*White female*	
Estimation equation	*(3.9)*	*(3.12)*	*(3.9)*	*(3.12)*	*(3.9)*	*(3.12)*
Differential						
Predicted Log Wage Rate: Cohort	3.1519***	3.1604***	3.1095***	3.1552***	3.2208***	3.2083***
	(0.0057)	(0.0064)	(0.0216)	(0.0412)	(0.0050)	(0.0036)
Unadjusted Difference	0.2214***	0.2130***	0.2639***	0.2181***	0.1526***	0.1651***
	(0.0058)	(0.0065)	(0.0217)	(0.0412)	(0.0051)	(0.0038)
Decomposition of Unadjusted Difference						
Portion Attributable to Endowments	0.0941***	0.0975***	0.0692***	0.0675***	−0.0053**	−0.0072***
	(0.0042)	(0.0048)	(0.0134)	(0.0252)	(0.0026)	(0.0020)
Portion Attributable to Coefficients	0.1160***	0.1037***	0.2095***	0.1563***	0.1489***	0.1597***
	(0.0057)	(0.0063)	(0.0216)	(0.0412)	(0.0051)	(0.0038)
Interaction (Simultaneously Attributed to Endowments and Coefficients)	0.0113***	0.0118***	−0.0148	−0.0057	0.0090***	0.0126***
	(0.0040)	(0.0046)	(0.0134)	(0.0251)	(0.0026)	(0.0021)

Note Differentials and decompositions correspond to results presented in Table 3.6

differences that are potentially attributable to discrimination are smaller for black males (11.6% and 10.37%) as compared to white females (14.89% and 15.97%) and black females (20.95% and 15.63%).

3.3 A Summary

We have presented our empirical strategy, and we have stressed the need for an analysis of intersectional wage discrimination. Estimating the Mincer equation via the application of the Blinder-Oaxaca decomposition technique while adjusting for possible sample selection bias, we have demonstrated statistically significant differences in predicted hourly wage rates between black workers and white workers and between female workers and their male counterparts. When comparing the white male worker null cohort to white female, black male, and black female worker groups, we again find that significant portions of the differences in predicted hourly wage rates cannot be explained solely by differences in productive characteristics, thus suggesting the presence of wage discrimination.

In the next chapter, we present estimates of wage discrimination for each of our worker groups that are defined based on their multiple intersecting identities (i.e., the personal characteristics of Hispanic ethnicity, nativity, race, and sex).

Appendices

Appendix A: Industry and Occupation Classifications

Industry Classifications

Agriculture, Forestry, Fishing, and Hunting; Arts, Entertainment, and Recreation, and Accommodation and Food Services; Construction; Educational Services; Finance and Insurance, and Real Estate and Rental and Leasing; Health Care; Information; Manufacturing; Mining, Quarrying, and Oil and Gas Extraction; Other Services, Except Public Administration; Professional, Scientific, and Management, and Administrative and Waste Management Services; Public Administration; Retail Trade; Social Assistance; Transportation and Warehousing; Utilities; Wholesale Trade.

Occupation Classifications
Architecture and Engineering Occupations; Arts, Design, Entertainment, Sports, and Media Occupations; Building and Grounds Cleaning and Maintenance Occupations; Business Operations Occupations; Community and Social Service Occupations; Computer and Mathematical Occupations; Construction Occupations; Educational Instruction, and Library Occupations; Extraction Occupations; Farming, Fishing, and Forestry Occupations; Financial Operations Occupations; Food Preparation and Serving Related Occupations; Healthcare Practitioners and Technical Occupations; Healthcare Support Occupations; Installation, Maintenance, and Repair Occupations; Legal Occupations; Life, Physical, and Social Science Occupations; Management Occupations; Office and Administrative Support Occupations; Personal Care and Service Occupations; Production Occupations; Protective Service Occupations; Sales and Office Occupations; Transportation and Material Moving Occupations.

Appendix B

Table 3.8 Heckman sample selection bias correction model results

Group	*Black* (*a*)	*Black female* (*b*)	*Black male* (*c*)	*White female* (*d*)
Education (in years)	0.0667***	0.0451***	0.0710***	0.0171***
	(0.0036)	(0.0056)	(0.0050)	(0.0026)
Age	0.0397***	0.0743***	0.0255***	0.1035***
	(0.0061)	(0.0098)	(0.0082)	(0.0046)
Age Squared	−0.0004***	−0.0009***	−0.0003***	−0.0013***
	(0.0001)	(0.0001)	(0.0001)	(0.0001)
English-speaking Household	−0.0995**	−0.0987	−0.1159**	0.0294
	(0.0391)	(0.0616)	(0.0519)	(0.0277)
Homeowner	0.4098***	0.1811***	0.5932***	0.1686***
	(0.0226)	(0.0343)	(0.0312)	(0.0169)
Kids 0–6 years of age in Household	0.1215***	−0.1245***	0.2813***	−0.1712***
	(0.0324)	(0.0428)	(0.0523)	(0.0203)
Kids 7–17 years of age in Household	0.3300***	0.0485	0.4858***	0.0166
	(0.0270)	(0.0371)	(0.0432)	(0.0176)
Married	0.1325***	−0.0389	0.2674***	−0.0939***
	(0.0268)	(0.0408)	(0.0371)	(0.0204)
Widowed, Divorced, or Separated	0.1261***	0.0042	0.2135***	−0.0139
	(0.0316)	(0.0466)	(0.0448)	(0.0251)
Constant	−0.1803***	−0.0373	−0.2070	−0.0292
	(0.1321)	(0.2088)	(0.1784)	(0.0954)
Inverse Mills Ratio	−0.6338***	−0.9770**	−0.5451***	−0.6189***
	(0.0643)	(0.3966)	(0.0463)	(0.1208)

Note Results for the black worker cohort correspond to Table 3.4. Results for all other cohorts correspond to Table 3.6. "***", "**", and "*" denote statistical significance from zero at the 1%, 5%, and 10% levels, respectively

References

Bauer, Thomas K., and Mathias Sinning. 2008. An Extension of the Blinder-Oaxaca Decomposition to Nonlinear Models. *Advances in Statistical Analysis* 92: 197–206.

Bauer, Thomas K., and Mathias Sinning. 2010. Blinder-Oaxaca Decomposition for Tobit Models. *Applied Economics* 42 (12): 1569–1575.

Becker, Gary S. 1994. *Human Capital: A Theoretical and Empirical Analysis with Special Reference to Education*, 3rd ed. Chicago, IL: University of Chicago Press.

Becker, Gary S. 2002. The Age of Human Capital. Online: Retrieved from https://www.hoover.org/sites/default/files/uploads/documents/0817928928_3.pdf.

Blank, Rebecca M. 1990. Are Part-Time Jobs Bad Jobs? In *A Future of Lousy Jobs? The Changing Structure of U.S. Wages*, ed. Gary Burtless, 123–155. Washington, DC: Brookings Institution.

Blinder, Alan. 1973. Wage Discrimination: Reduced Form and Structural Estimates. *Journal of Human Resources* 8 (4): 436–455.

Cotton, Jeremiah. 1988. On the Decomposition of Wage Differentials. *Review of Economics and Statistics* 70 (2): 236–243.

Dell'Aringa, Carlo, Claudio Lucifora, and Laura Pagani. 2015. Earnings Differentials between Immigrants and Natives: The Role of Occupational Attainment. *IZA Journal of Migration* 4 (8): 1–18.

Fadlon, Yariv D. 2015. Statistical Discrimination and the Implication of Employer-Employee Racial Matches. *Journal of Labor Research* 36 (2): 232–248.

Fairlie, Robert W. 2005. An Extension of the Blinder-Oaxaca Decomposition Technique to Logit and Probit Models. *Journal of Economic and Social Measurement* 30 (4): 305–316.

Fortin, Nicole, Thomas Lemieux, and Sergio Firpo. 2010. Decomposition Methods in Economics. NBER Working Paper No. 16045. Cambridge, MA: National Bureau of Economic Research.

Heckman, James J. 1976. The Common Structure of Statistical Models of Truncation, Sample Selection and Limited Dependent Variables and a Simple Estimator for Such Models. *Annals of Econometrics and Social Measurement* 5 (4): 475–492.

Heckman, James J. 1979. Sample Selection Bias as a Specification Error. *Econometrica* 47: 153–161.

Heckman, James J. 1990. Selection Bias and Self-selection. In *The New Palgrave: Econometrics*, ed. John Eatwell, Murray Milgate, and Peter Newman, 201–224. New York: Norton.

Hirsch, Barry T. 2005. Why Do Part-Time Workers Earn Less? The Role of Worker and Job Skill. *Industrial and Labor Relations Review* 58 (4): 525–551.

Jann, Ben. 2008. The Blinder-Oaxaca Decomposition for Linear Regression Models. *The Stata Journal* 8 (4): 453–479.

Jolly, Nicholas A. 2012. Job Displacement and the Inter-temporal Movement of Workers through the Earnings and Income Distributions. *Contemporary Economic Policy* 31 (2): 392–406.

Mincer, Jacob. 1958. Investment in Human Capital and Personal Income Distribution. *Journal of Political Economy* 66 (4): 281–302.

Mincer, Jacob. 1974. *Schooling, Experience, and Earnings*. Cambridge, MA: National Bureau of Economic Research.

Neumark, David. 1988. Employers' Discriminatory Behavior and the Estimation of Wage Discrimination. *Journal of Human Resources* 23 (3): 279–295.

Oaxaca, Ronald. 1973. Male-Female Wage Differentials in Urban Labor Markets. *International Economic Review* 14 (3): 693–709.

Oaxaca, Ronald L., and Michael R. Ransom. 1994. On Discrimination and the Decomposition of Wage Differentials. *Journal of Econometrics* 61 (1): 5–21.

Rosen, Sherwin. 1992. Distinguished Fellow: Mincering Labor Economics. *Journal of Economic Perspectives* 6 (2): 157–170.

Willis, Robert J. 1986. Wage Determinants: A Survey and Reinterpretation of Human Capital Earnings Functions. In *The Handbook of Labor Economics*, ed. Orley C. Ashenfelter and Richard Layard, vol. 1: 525–602.

Yun, Myeong-Su. 2004. Decomposing Differences in the First Moment. *Economics Letters* 82 (2): 273–278.

Part II

CHAPTER 4

Estimating Wage Discrimination and Examining Variation Across Worker Groups

Abstract We use the Blinder-Oaxaca decomposition technique and a Heckman sample selection correction model to estimate variants of the Mincer earnings function. This results in estimated wage discrimination rates for each worker group. The groups are defined based on unique combinations of workers' personal characteristics (i.e., Hispanic ethnicity, nativity, race, and sex). Generating estimated discrimination rates is an essential step toward determining whether wage discrimination in the US labor market is intersectional. To estimate wage discrimination, we compare 43 worker groups, in turn, to our null worker cohort which is comprised of native-born, non-Hispanic, white, male workers. In the typical year during our 2008–2020 reference period, we examine data for 882,342 workers, and over our entire reference period, we examine data for 11,470,451 workers. Given that we estimate four regression models for each of our 43 worker groups for each of the 13 years in our reference period, in total, we produce more than 2,200 wage discrimination estimates.

Keywords Estimated wage discrimination · Hispanic ethnicity · Nativity · Race · Sex · Worker groups

R. White, *Intersectionality and Discrimination*,
https://doi.org/10.1007/978-3-031-26125-1_4

The estimation of wage discrimination rates for each of the 43 worker groups in our study is an essential step toward identifying intersectional wage discrimination. We follow the empirical strategy that is presented and discussed in Chapter 3 to produce our estimated discrimination rates. As is noted, this process involves estimating our battery of Mincer earnings functions while using the Blinder-Oaxaca decomposition technique to compare each of our worker groups, in turn, to our null cohort of native-born, non-Hispanic, white, male workers. We begin with a complete ACS data file for 2008, the first year in our reference period.[1] We then restrict the data set to include only those individuals 16–64 years of age who worked more than 32 hours in the typical week during the past 12 months. We also exclude self-employed individuals, active-duty members of the military, and any observations for which the potential labor force experience variable is less than zero.[2] Thus, in the typical year during our 2008–2020 reference period, we examine data for 882,342 workers, and over the 13-year reference period, our full sample represents 11,470,451 workers.

To identify the presence and extent of wage discrimination for each worker group, we first reduce our full data sample such that it includes only those observations that comprise our null cohort of native-born, non-Hispanic, white male workers. We then add the observations that correspond with a single worker group (e.g., native-born, non-Hispanic, white female workers). By estimating Eqs. 3.9–3.12 while using the Blinder-Oaxaca decomposition technique and the Heckman sample selection model (i.e., Eq. 3.15), we identify the unexplained portions of the predicted hourly wage gap between our null worker cohort and the worker group being considered.

We then repeat these steps, retaining the observations for our null worker cohort and a second worker group (e.g., native-born, non-Hispanic, black male workers). By again estimating our battery of Mincer

[1] The data files we examine are year-specific and include both the ACS population data and corresponding household data.

[2] In all estimations, our measure of potential labor market experience is constructed as the worker's age minus their years of schooling minus six. Thus, if the experience variable is negative, then the survey respondent must be understating their age and/or overstating their years of education. Based on the rationale that if the respondent is either unwilling or unable to accurately report their age and/or education, they are also likely unwilling or unable to accurately report other information, we exclude these individuals from our data.

earnings functions, we obtain estimates of potential wage discrimination (i.e., the unexplained portion of the wage gap between our null worker cohort and this second worker group). This process is repeated until we produce estimates of wage discrimination for each of the 43 worker groups in our data set for each of the 13 years in our reference period. Since we estimate four earnings functions for each year in our reference period, we obtain as many as 52 estimates of potential wage discrimination for each worker group.[3] Thus, in total, we generate more than 2,200 estimates of potential wage discrimination. In the next section, we present our findings. Later in this chapter, we consider variation in estimated worker group-specific discrimination rates across time.

Before detailing our findings, it is important to again stress that we do not have a "discrimination" variable; thus, we cannot simply examine the statistical significance of the corresponding coefficient estimate to determine whether discrimination is present. Instead, we employ the Blinder-Oaxaca decomposition technique, and if some portion of the gap in predicted hourly wages between a worker group and our null worker cohort remains unexplained, we have evidence of potential wage discrimination. As discussed in section 1.3, researchers who examine wage discrimination typically practice great caution when interpreting results and, thus, are generally reluctant to attribute the unexplained portion of the wage gap to discrimination. We chose to break with this convention and label the unexplained portion of the wage gap as wage discrimination. The rationale for breaking with convention is simply that, given the gravity of our subject, we consider the risk of overstating wage discrimination to be less of a concern than possibly understating the extent of discrimination and, by doing so, de-emphasizing the problem.

4.1 Estimates of Potential Wage Discrimination During 2020

We begin our discussion by focusing on results obtained from the evaluation of ACS data from 2020, the most recent year for which data are available. Figure 4.1 summarizes the estimated wage discrimination rates for this year. The horizontal bars in the figure represent estimates of wage

[3] As noted earlier, we limit our analysis to exclude estimations involving fewer than 250 observations.

discrimination that (i) correspond to our four Mincer earnings functions and (ii) are statistically significant from zero. The worker groups associated with the sets of bars (i.e., the estimated discrimination rates) are listed in the leftmost column of the figure. For example, the first set of bars in the figure corresponds to the "fb, h, b, f" worker group. This group includes foreign-born, Hispanic, black, female workers. Similarly, the second set of bars corresponds to the "fb, h, w, f" group (i.e., foreign-born, Hispanic, white, female workers), etc. The values immediately to the right of the worker group abbreviations are the simple average of the estimated discrimination rate values that are represented by the bars. The values in parentheses to the right of the average estimated discrimination rates are the number of earnings functions estimations for which statistically significant discrimination rates are obtained. Since there are four earnings functions, the maximum possible value is four.

The first group listed in the figure has an average discrimination rate for 2020 of 0.2734; however, only one of the four Mincer equation estimations yielded a statistically significant discrimination rate. For the second group listed, the average estimated discrimination rate is equal to 0.2672 and each of the four earnings functions produced a discrimination rate that is statistically significant from zero. These two values indicate that even once accounting for the explained portion of the difference in predicted hourly wage rates, the typical workers in these groups face unexplained wage gaps of 27.34% and 26.72%, respectively. Stated differently, seemingly due to wage discrimination, in 2020, the typical foreign-born, Hispanic, black, female worker was paid an hourly wage rate that was more than 27% less than the amount paid to a comparable native-born, non-Hispanic, white, male worker. Likewise, the typical foreign-born, Hispanic, white female worker was paid almost 27% less than a comparable native-born, non-Hispanic, white, male worker. Here, "comparable" indicates that the workers possess the same productive characteristics (i.e., same levels of education and potential labor force experience) and the same occupation classification, industry of employment, and state of residence as the typical member of the null worker cohort.

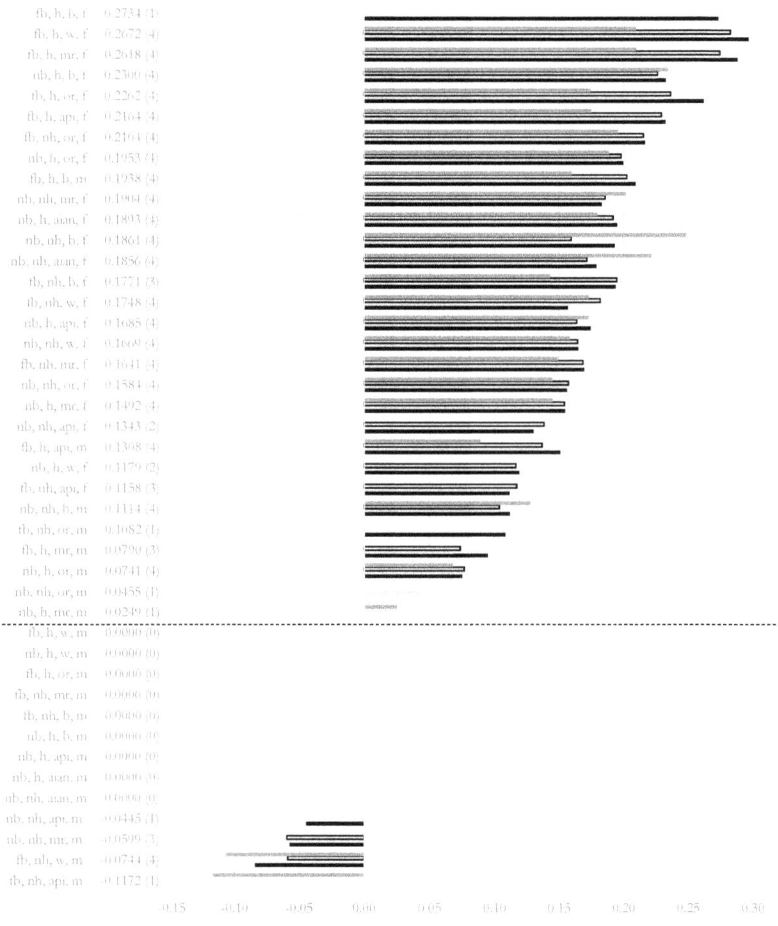

Fig. 4.1 Estimates of wage discrimination in 2020, relative to the native-born, non-Hispanic, white, male null worker cohort (*Note* fb = foreign-born, "nb" = native-born, "h" = Hispanic, "nh" = non-Hispanic, "f" = female, "m" = male, "aian" = American Indian or Alaska native, "api" = Asian or Pacific Islander, "b" = black, "mr" = multiple races, "or" = other race, and "w" =white)

The worker groups are presented in descending order based on the average value of the statistically significant discrimination rate estimates.[4,5] The mean average value across the worker groups, including the values that are equal to zero and those that are negative, is 10.77%. The median average value is 13.08%. There are nine worker groups for which no wage discrimination is identified (i.e., average values of zero) and another four groups for which the average estimated discrimination rate is negative. These worker groups are listed below the dotted horizontal line. Somewhat surprisingly, not one of these 13 groups includes female workers. With respect to Hispanic ethnicity, nativity, and race classifications, the 13 groups are quite evenly mixed. For example, six groups include Hispanic workers while seven groups include non-Hispanic workers. Similarly, six groups include foreign-born workers, and seven groups are comprised of native-born workers. Two race classifications (i.e., the Asian or Pacific Islander and white classifications) each appear three times among these 13 worker groups, yet every other race classification appears twice except for the other race classification which appears only once. Similarly, there are no overly common combinations of personal characteristics among these groups.

Each of the remaining 30 worker groups for which positive and statistically significant average estimated discrimination rates have been obtained has a positive average estimated discrimination rate. The average values range from a low of 2.49% for the native-born, Hispanic, multiple race, male worker group to the aforementioned 27.34% for the foreign-born, Hispanic, black, female worker group. To examine the personal characteristics of the worker groups, in Fig. 4.2, we order the average discrimination rates in descending order from left to right along the x-axis. The graph in the top portion of the figure illustrates the cumulative frequencies for three personal characteristics: Hispanic ethnicity, foreign-born, and female. The abbreviations along the x-axis that correspond to the average discrimination rate values indicate the race of the workers in the associated group. For example, the sixth value from the left along the

4 Appendix Table 4.2 provides a comprehensive list of estimated discrimination rates, whether statistically significant from zero or not, for each estimation equation and worker group.

5 Although our analysis is focused on workers engaged in full-time employment, we report estimated discrimination rates for part-time workers, for the year 2020, in Appendix Table 4.3.

x-axis is 0.2164. This is the average estimated discrimination rate for the foreign-born, Hispanic, Asian or Pacific Islander, female worker group. Accordingly, to denote the race classification, we have placed "api" on the x-axis preceding the value.

Because the Hispanic, foreign-born, and female characteristics are binary—that is, if a worker is not foreign-born, then they are native-born, and if they are not Hispanic, they are non-Hispanic, and if they are not

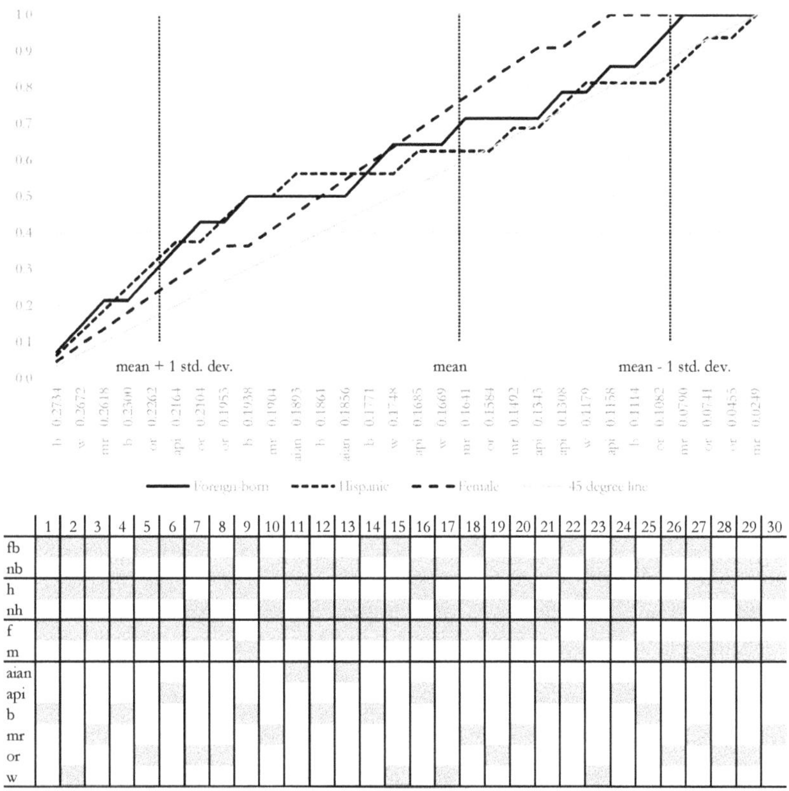

Fig. 4.2 Average estimated discrimination rates with cumulative frequencies and worker group characteristics, 2020 (*Note* Only positive and statistically significant mean values are reported here. See Table 4.2 in the appendix for a listing of all statistically significant values for each estimation equation. See Fig. 4.1 notes for an explanation of abbreviations)

female, they are male—a 45-degree line has been added to the graph to better indicate the disproportionate representation of Hispanic, foreign-born, and especially female workers in the groups that have higher average estimated discrimination rates. Similarly, the columns in the bottom portion of the figure correspond to the 30 worker groups represented in the graph with the shaded squares identifying the personal characteristics of each worker group. This facilitates the identification of commonalities in personal characteristics across worker groups and permits average discrimination rates to be more easily identified. For example, mirroring the cumulative distributions presented in the graph, we see that being foreign-born, Hispanic, and/or female are common personal characteristics among the worker groups with the higher average discrimination rate values.

Beginning with the foreign-born characteristic and focusing on the graph, the portions of the heavy solid line that slope upward indicate that the corresponding worker group includes foreign-born individuals. Segments of the line that are horizontal correspond with worker groups that include native-born workers. Thus, the y-axis value indicates the cumulative frequency of groups that include foreign-born individuals. While only 14 of the 30 workers groups depicted in the graph include foreign-born workers, we see from the shaded areas in the bottom portion of the figure that seven of the nine highest estimated average discrimination rates are found for groups that include foreign-born workers. Thus, the cumulative frequency value for the foreign-born personal characteristic reaches 50% at the ninth worker group from the origin.

The cumulative frequency of the Hispanic ethnicity characteristic follows a similar initial path. Specifically, nine of the 11 groups with the highest average discrimination rates include Hispanic workers. Even more pronounced is the line which represents the female worker characteristic. With two exceptions, the line continually slopes upward through the first 24 worker cohorts presented in the graph. This reflects the fact that, as is shown in the bottom portion of the figure, 22 of the 24 worker groups with the highest discrimination rates include female workers. Conversely, the groups that include male workers have lower estimated average discrimination rates or are not shown in this figure (i.e., have estimated values of zero or that are negative).

With respect to race, the picture is less clear. We see that groups that include black workers appear quite frequently (i.e., five times) in the top half of average discrimination rate values (i.e., among the highest 15 estimated rates). We also see that groups comprised of workers who identify as other race appear three times in the highest 15. Thus, these two race classifications collectively account for more than one-half of the highest 15 values. To the contrary, no groups that include white male workers have a single positive and statistically significant estimated discrimination rates. Additionally, all groups that include white female workers have one or more positive and statistically significant discrimination rate. Finally, of the five worker groups with the lowest average estimated discrimination rates, three groups include individuals who self-identify as other race. In each of these cases, the groups include male workers. The remaining worker group which includes workers of some other race and that has a positive and statistically significant average estimated discrimination rate includes female workers and is ranked 19th of the 30 groups.

4.2 Variation in Estimated Wage Discrimination Rates, 2008–2020

Figure 4.3 illustrates the time paths of estimated discrimination rates for each worker group in our study.[6] Each line represents the three-year moving average of estimated discrimination rates that are obtained when estimating Eq. 3.9. There are six panels in the figure, each of which corresponds to a different race classification. For example, panel A illustrates the time-specific values for the American Indian and Alaska native worker groups, panel B illustrates the values for the Asian or Pacific Islander worker groups, etc. Regardless of race classification (i.e., panel), the corresponding null worker cohort is comprised of native-born, non-Hispanic, white, male workers. For example, in panel A, we see that during the 2008–2010 period, the average estimated discrimination rate for the native-born, non-Hispanic, American Indian and Alaska native worker group is 20.76%.

A review of the panels reveals several interesting relationships. First, consistent with the findings presented in Figs. 4.1 and 4.2, discrimination rates for groups that include female workers are consistently higher than the rates for groups that include male workers. In fact, in panels A, D,

[6] The values illustrated in Fig. 4.3 are calculated from the values presented in Appendix Table 4.4, which lists the full set of estimated discrimination rates for each worker group and each estimation equation in our study.

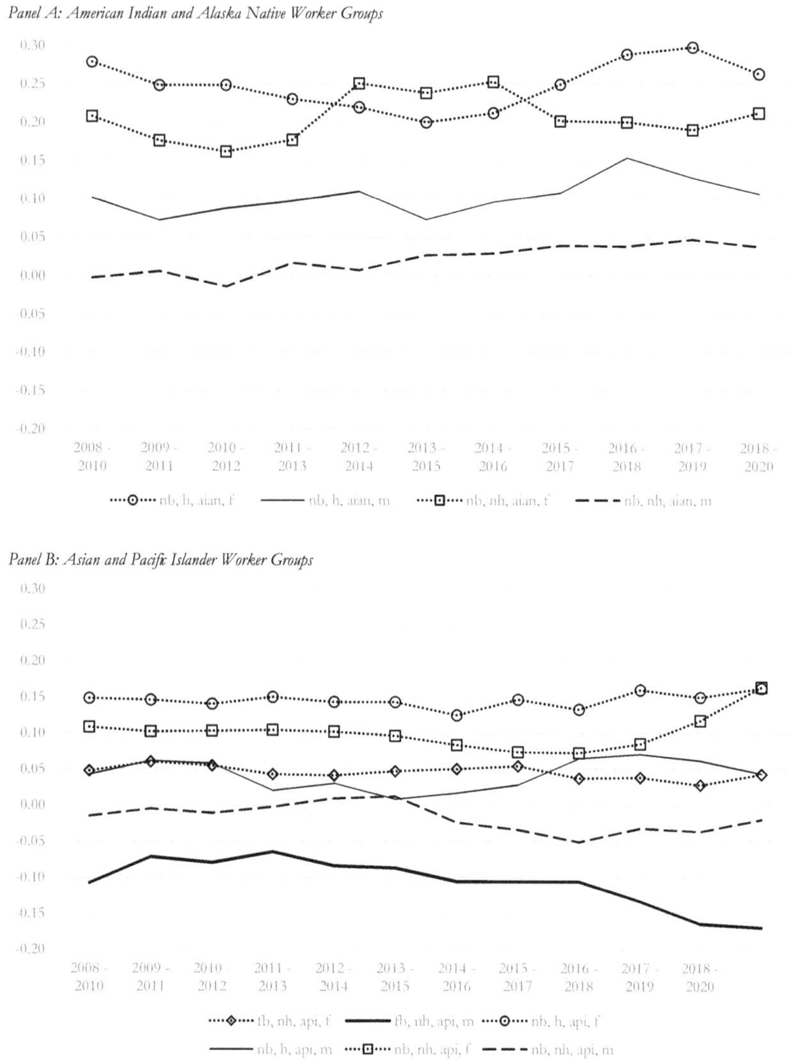

Fig. 4.3 Time paths (three-year moving averages) of estimated wage discrimination rates (Eq. 3.9) (*Note* See Fig. 4.1 notes for an explanation of abbreviations

Panel C: Black Worker Groups

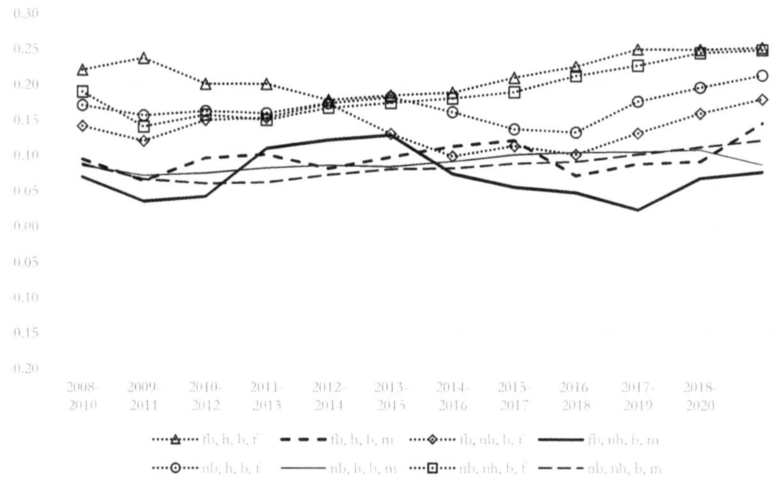

Panel D: Multiple Races Worker Groups

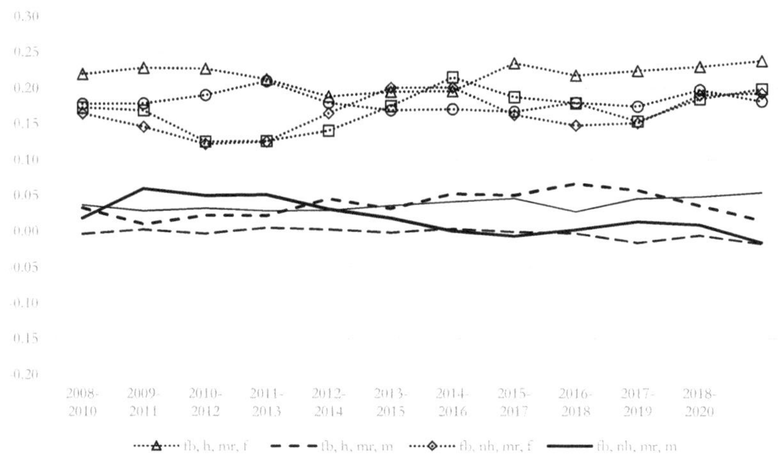

Fig. 4.3 (continued)

Panel E: Other Race Worker Groups

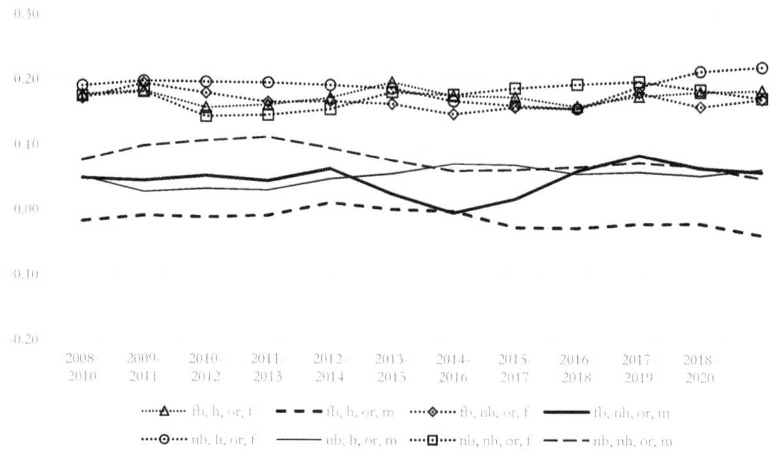

Panel F: White Worker Groups

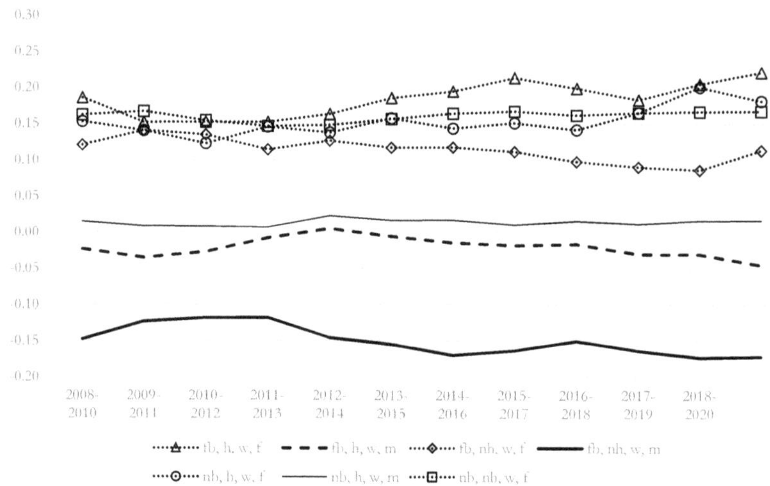

Fig. 4.3 (continued)

E, and F, the estimated values for all worker groups comprised of female workers are higher than all corresponding values for male worker groups. Similar, although less pronounced, patterns are found in the remaining two panels. Second, we also see that, in a large majority of instances, the estimated values for groups that include Hispanic workers are higher than those reported for groups comprised of non-Hispanic workers. To the contrary, we do not see such clear differences with respect to the nativity or race classifications.

We find additional interesting results when reviewing the year-specific discrimination rate values that are presented in Appendix Table 4.4. Comparison of average estimated discrimination rates across pairs of worker groups that differ only by sex, we see that in 22 of 22 instances, the value is higher for the groups that include female workers rather than the male worker groups. In most instances, the differences are quite large. For example, the average discrimination rate for the native-born, non-Hispanic, black, female worker group is 19%. This is more than twice the value reported for the native-born, non-Hispanic, black, male worker group. Similarly, the average discrimination rate for the foreign-born, Hispanic, multiple race, female worker group is 21.91%, while the value for the foreign-born, Hispanic, multiple race, male worker group is only 3.23%. A similar comparison of the average estimated discrimination rate across pairs of worker groups that differ only by Hispanic ethnicity reveals that in 17 of 22 instances (77.3%), the value is higher for the groups that include Hispanic workers. Lastly, comparing across pairs of worker groups that differ by nativity, we see that worker groups that include foreign-born workers have higher rates in only 9 of 20 instances (45%).

Thus far, our results strongly suggest that there is greater discrimination toward female workers and Hispanic workers relative to their male and non-Hispanic counterparts. With respect to nativity and race, the patterns are far less clear. Since our null worker cohort consists of native-born, non-Hispanic, white, male workers, another point of comparison is to consider average estimated discrimination rates across worker groups that are categorized by the number of differences in personal characteristics relative to the null worker cohort.

Of the 43 worker groups for which discrimination rates have been calculated, eight groups differ from our null worker cohort in only one characteristic (e.g., native-born, non-Hispanic, white, female workers or foreign-born, non-Hispanic, white, male workers). Only four worker groups differ from the null cohort in all four characteristics. This group

Table 4.1 Average estimated discrimination rates, by number of differences in personal characteristics

Number of different characteristics	*Number of worker groups*	*Average discrimination rate*
1	8	0.0241
2	17	0.0852
3	14	0.1312
4	4	0.2059

includes foreign-born, Hispanic, female workers who are either Asian or Pacific Islander, black, multiple races, or some other race. Seventeen groups differ from the null worker cohort in two personal characteristics (e.g., the native-born, non-Hispanic, American Indian or Alaska native, female worker group), and 14 groups differ in three personal characteristics (e.g., the foreign-born, Hispanic, multiple race, male worker group). The average estimated discrimination rates for these groups are presented in Table 4.1.

Consistent with the results presented in this chapter, we see that, on average, worker groups comprised of individuals who differ from our null worker cohort in more personal characteristics experience higher rates of wage discrimination. The average discrimination rate among the worker groups that differ from the null cohort in all four personal characteristics is 20.59%. Very much to the contrary, the average estimated discrimination rate among worker groups that differ from the null cohort in a single characteristic is equal to only 2.41%. Worker groups that differ from the null cohort in three characteristics have an average discrimination rate of 13.12%, and the average estimated discrimination rate across worker groups that differ from the null cohort in two characteristics is 8.52%. Lastly, across the 43 worker groups, the pairwise correlation coefficient between the number of personal characteristic differences and the average estimated discrimination rate is equal to 0.30, again indicating that workers that are more different in terms of personal characteristics from the null worker cohort generally experience higher discrimination rates.

4.3 A Summary

In this chapter, we have presented estimated discrimination rates for each of our 43 worker groups. Focusing first on discrimination rates obtained when examining data from 2020, we find considerable variation across worker groups with higher discrimination rates generally found for groups that include Hispanic, foreign-born, and/or female workers. This same general pattern is reported—especially with respect to groups that include female workers—when we consider the time paths of discrimination rates for each worker group over our 2008–2020 reference period. We also find that estimated discrimination rates are generally higher for worker groups that are more different from the null worker cohort in terms of personal characteristics.

Having produced estimated discrimination rates, in the following chapter, we calculate expected discrimination rates and compare our estimated and expected values to determine if wage discrimination in the U.S. labor market is intersectional. We conclude our examination by exploring potential pre-labor market discrimination that may affect workers' subsequent wages, and we compare the patterns of estimated discrimination rates that are reported here to worker group-specific returns to schooling.

Appendix

Table 4.2 Estimated wage discrimination rates—full-time workers, 2020

	AIAN	*API*	*Black*	*Mult. races*	*Other race*	*White*
Panel A: Estimation equation (3.9)						
nb, nh, m	−0.0047	0.0094	0.1279***	−0.0435	0.0312	a
nb, h, m	0.0537	0.0096	0.0151	0.0249**	0.068***	0.0189
fb, nh, m	b	−0.1172*	0.0695	−0.0392	0.0653	−0.107***
fb, h, m	b	0.089**	0.16***	0.0014	−0.0899	−0.0651
nb, nh, f	0.2217***	0.2266	0.2485***	0.2015***	0.1451***	0.1583***
nb, h, f	0.1797***	0.1729***	0.2347***	0.1451***	0.1886***	0.0964
fb, nh, f	b	0.071	0.1431*	0.1496***	0.1956***	0.173***
fb, h, f	b	0.175***	0.2491	0.2097***	0.1742***	0.2095***
Panel B: Estimation equation (3.10)						
nb, nh, m	−0.0167	−0.051	0.1035***	−0.0595*	0.0423	a
nb, h, m	0.051	0.0389	0.0218	0.0213	0.0766***	0.0028
fb, nh, m	b	−0.0795	0.1076	−0.0345	0.1043	−0.0588***
fb, h, m	b	0.1367***	0.2024***	0.0735**	0.0354	0.0235
nb, nh, f	0.1716***	0.1383*	0.1594***	0.1857***	0.1573***	0.1644***
nb, h, f	0.1917***	0.1637***	0.2265***	0.1541***	0.1979***	0.1165*
fb, nh, f	b	0.117***	0.1945***	0.1686***	0.2155***	0.1818***
fb, h, f	b	0.2295***	0.2612	0.2745***	0.2368***	0.2825***

	AIAN	*API*	*Black*	*Mult. races*	*Other race*	*White*
Panel C: Estimation equation (3.11)						
nb, nh, m	−0.0163	−0.051	0.1025***	−0.0629*	0.0455*	a
nb, h, m	0.0511	0.0399	0.0207	0.0202	0.0767***	0.0029
fb, nh, m	b	−0.0769	0.1122	−0.0356	0.0968	−0.0478***
fb, h, m	b	0.1464***	0.2034***	0.0689**	0.0364	0.0249
nb, nh, f	0.1699***	0.1527	0.1432**	0.1913***	0.1748***	0.18***
nb, h, f	0.1911***	0.163***	0.2257***	0.1427***	0.1947***	0.0695
fb, nh, f	b	0.119***	0.1306	0.1686***	0.2139***	0.1874***
fb, h, f	b	0.2285***	0.2614	0.2749***	0.2314***	0.28***
Panel D: Estimation equation (3.12)						
nb, nh, m	−0.0144	−0.0445*	0.1118***	−0.0572*	0.0383	a
nb, h, m	0.0459	0.041	0.0208	0.0212	0.0752***	0.0076
fb, nh, m	b	−0.0893	0.109	−0.036	0.1082*	−0.0841***
fb, h, m	b	0.1509***	0.2094***	0.0946***	0.0729	0.0449
nb, nh, f	0.1791***	0.1302***	0.1931***	0.183***	0.1562***	0.1649***
nb, h, f	0.1948***	0.1745***	0.233***	0.1549***	0.1998***	0.1192*
fb, nh, f	b	0.1115***	0.1937***	0.1694***	0.2167***	0.1569***
fb, h, f	b	0.2327***	0.2734	0.2881***	0.2623***	0.2968***

Note a = null worker cohort. b = fewer than 250 observations for the worker group; thus, no estimations performed. See Fig. 4.1 notes for an explanation of abbreviations

Table 4.3 Estimated wage discrimination rates—part-time workers, 2020

	AIAN	*API*	*Black*	*Mult. races*	*Other race*	*White*
Panel A: Estimation equation (3.9)						
nb, nh, m	0.0225	0.0411	−0.0205	−0.0421	0.0162	a
nb, h, m	0.2246	−0.0188	0.154***	0.1362**	0.1981**	0.0952***
fb, nh, m	−0.0372	−0.1073	0.029	−0.0515	0.069**	0.0461
fb, h, m	0.225*	−0.0755	0.029	0.23***	0.2433**	0.0574
nb, nh, f	b	−0.351***	−0.1671**	0.2788	b	−0.1688**
nb, h, f	b	−0.2253	0.1604**	−0.0094	0.0286	0.1258**
fb, nh, f	b	b	b	−0.1627**	−0.1885***	−0.0016
fb, h, f	b	b	0.0361	0.1429**	0.0864	0.2067
Panel B: Estimation equation (3.10)						
nb, nh, m	−0.0484	0.0665	−0.0337	−0.0642	−0.038	a
nb, h, m	0.1883	0.0183	0.2087***	0.141**	0.1961**	0.106***
fb, nh, m	−0.0378	0.029	0.0183	−0.065	0.0681**	0.0455
fb, h, m	0.1938**	−0.1021	0.0314	0.2189***	0.2573**	0.1063
nb, nh, f	b	−0.1474***	−0.1583**	0.2569	b	−0.1469**
nb, h, f	b	0.0792	0.159**	0.0145	0.0713	0.1619***
fb, nh, f	b	b	b	−0.077	−0.0823	0.0767
fb, h, f	b	b	0.3018	0.1803***	0.1873**	0.2189

	AIAN	*API*	*Black*	*Mult. races*	*Other race*	*White*
Panel C: Estimation equation (3.11)						
nb, nh, m	−0.0503	0.0592	−0.0343	−0.0683	−0.0389	a
nb, h, m	0.2011	−0.0077	0.2888	0.0661	0.2065**	0.1308***
fb, nh, m	−0.037	0.0183	0.0082	−0.062	0.07**	0.0652
fb, h, m	0.1576**	−0.0996	0.0254	0.1772***	0.2423*	0.1235
nb, nh, f	b	−0.1114*	−0.1707**	0.2433	b	−0.1431**
nb, h, f	b	0.2675	0.134**	0.0283	0.1203	0.1662***
fb, nh, f	b	b	b	−0.0852	−0.0894	0.0602
fb, h, f	b	b	0.1429**	0.1719***	0.1937**	0.2057
Panel D: Estimation equation (3.12)						
nb, nh, m	−0.0211	0.073	−0.0327	−0.0759	0.0223	a
nb, h, m	0.1324	−0.0029	0.1738***	0.1414**	0.1557**	0.0927***
fb, nh, m	−0.0218	0.0082	0.0286	−0.0454	0.0745**	−0.028
fb, h, m	0.1412**	−0.1691	0.0398	0.2054***	0.2493**	0.091
nb, nh, f	b	−0.1963***	−0.1795**	0.2584	b	−0.1721***
nb, h, f	b	0.041	0.1361***	−0.0324	0.0497	0.1539**
fb, nh, f	b	b	b	−0.069	−0.0722	0.0774
fb, h, f	b	b	0.1803***	0.1748***	0.1853**	0.1852**

Note See Appendix Table 4.2 notes

Table 4.4 Annual estimates of wage discrimination, relative to the null worker cohort (i.e., native-born, non-Hispanic, white, male workers)

Panel A: Equation 3.9

Worker group	*2008*	*2009*	*2010*	*2011*	*2012*	*2013*	*2014*
nb, nh, aian, m	−0.0051	0.0600	−0.0635	0.0199	0.0004	0.0285	−0.0078
nb, nh, api, m	0.0196	−0.0337	−0.0019	0.0022	−0.0080	0.0326	0.0104
nb, nh, b, m	0.0844	0.0752	0.0390	0.0665	0.0806	0.0695	0.0908
nb, nh, mr, m	0.0283	−0.0285	0.0073	0.0110	−0.0038	0.0007	−0.0026
nb, nh, or, m	0.1029	0.0611	0.1315	0.1269	0.0778	0.0797	0.0705
nb, nh, aian, f	0.1826	0.2446	0.1956	0.0881	0.2015	0.2409	0.3091
nb, nh, api, f	0.1074	0.0969	0.1020	0.1097	0.1013	0.0941	0.0917
nb, nh, b, f	0.0971	0.1811	0.1441	0.1464	0.1598	0.1948	0.1672
nb, nh, mr, f	0.2115	0.1183	0.1756	0.0816	0.1209	0.2190	0.1842
nb, nh, or, f	0.2011	0.1845	0.1588	0.0876	0.1915	0.1851	0.1666
nb, nh, w, f	0.1828	0.1673	0.1498	0.1453	0.1439	0.1543	0.1717
nb, h, aian, m	0.1307	0.1029	0.0696	0.0437	0.1495	0.0976	0.0814
nb, h, api, m	0.0312	0.1289	0.0236	0.0199	0.0167	0.0533	−0.0464
nb, h, b, m	0.0655	0.0716	0.0777	0.0746	0.0948	0.0878	0.0684
nb, h, mr, m	0.0304	0.0294	0.0247	0.0416	0.0190	0.0257	0.0625
nb, h, or, m	0.0407	0.0208	0.0216	0.0549	0.0138	0.0742	0.0778
nb, h, w, m	0.0230	0.0182	−0.0171	0.0210	0.0152	0.0299	0.0027
nb, h, aian, f	0.2965	0.2690	0.2696	0.2053	0.2697	0.2145	0.1734
nb, h, api, f	0.1944	0.1382	0.1052	0.1772	0.1667	0.0851	0.1763
nb, h, b, f	0.1532	0.1763	0.1398	0.1717	0.1667	0.1822	0.1963
nb, h, mr, f	0.1509	0.1529	0.2306	0.1860	0.2123	0.1391	0.1555
nb, h, or, f	0.2005	0.1894	0.2035	0.1962	0.1856	0.1932	0.1817
nb, h, w, f	0.1757	0.1194	0.1255	0.1224	0.1891	0.1016	0.1817

Panel A: Equation 3.9

Worker group	*2008*	*2009*	*2010*	*2011*	*2012*	*2013*	*2014*
fb, nh, api, m	−0.0683	−0.1010	−0.0456	−0.0919	−0.0569	−0.1030	−0.1021
fb, nh, b, m	0.0253	0.0367	0.0434	0.0459	0.2405	0.0792	0.0665
fb, nh, mr, m	0.0741	0.0363	0.0665	0.0461	0.0391	0.0071	0.0076
fb, nh, or, m	0.0473	0.1055	−0.0185	0.0695	0.0821	0.0379	−0.0465
fb, nh, w, m	−0.1393	−0.1198	−0.1114	−0.1245	−0.1184	−0.1945	−0.1514
fb, nh, api, f	0.0770	0.0653	0.0374	0.0607	0.0287	0.0331	0.0778
fb, nh, b, f	0.1569	0.1304	0.0741	0.2451	0.1413	0.1324	0.1182
fb, nh, mr, f	0.1505	0.1458	0.1415	0.0782	0.1558	0.2603	0.1853
fb, nh, or, f	0.2245	0.1928	0.1655	0.1799	0.1516	0.1697	0.1679
fb, nh, w, f	0.1784	0.1461	0.0970	0.1603	0.0854	0.1328	0.1322
fb, h, api, m	.	0.0542	0.0178	.	0.0435	0.0861	0.1391
fb, h, b, m	0.0034	0.0792	0.1095	0.0993	0.0955	0.0488	0.1489
fb, h, mr, m	0.0181	0.0234	−0.0128	0.0548	0.0225	0.0573	0.0148
fb, h, or, m	0.0041	−0.0017	−0.0283	−0.0042	0.0059	0.0309	−0.0347
fb, h, w, m	−0.0189	−0.0345	−0.0530	0.0053	0.0228	−0.0142	−0.0267
fb, h, api, f	0.1563	0.3248	0.1221	0.2063	.	.	0.2746
fb, h, b, f	0.2833	0.1977	0.2304	0.1741	0.1979	0.1622	0.1933
fb, h, mr, f	0.2198	0.2392	0.2246	0.2162	0.1957	0.1524	0.2363
fb, h, or, f	0.2146	0.1786	0.1561	0.1367	0.1910	0.1891	0.2084
fb, h, w, f	0.1359	0.1902	0.1291	0.1373	0.1903	0.1620	0.2037

(continued)

Table 4.4 (continued)

Panel A: Equation 3.9

Worker group	*2015*	*2016*	*2017*	*2018*	*2019*	*2020*
nb, nh, aian, m	0.0580	0.0364	0.0234	0.0548	0.0627	−0.0047
nb, nh, api, m	−0.1154	0.0022	−0.0409	−0.0582	−0.0125	0.0094
nb, nh, b, m	0.0839	0.0891	0.0999	0.1149	0.1201	0.1279
nb, nh, mr, m	0.0125	−0.0132	−0.0085	−0.0271	0.0171	−0.0435
nb, nh, or, m	0.0297	0.0836	0.0841	0.0506	0.0636	0.0312
nb, nh, aian, f	0.1635	0.2855	0.1555	0.1598	0.2549	0.2217
nb, nh, api, f	0.0643	0.0638	0.0881	0.1026	0.1602	0.2266
nb, nh, b, f	0.1784	0.2214	0.2354	0.2221	0.2737	0.2485
nb, nh, mr, f	0.2414	0.1356	0.1596	0.1651	0.2291	0.2015
nb, nh, or, f	0.1791	0.2158	0.1840	0.1923	0.1780	0.1451
nb, nh, w, f	0.1656	0.1636	0.1559	0.1755	0.1686	0.1583
nb, h, aian, m	0.0391	0.1664	0.1172	0.1777	0.0877	0.0537
nb, h, api, m	0.0429	0.0867	0.0637	0.0602	0.0590	0.0096
nb, h, b, m	0.1182	0.1163	0.0783	0.1199	0.1253	0.0151
nb, h, mr, m	0.0356	0.0390	0.0069	0.0898	0.0464	0.0249
nb, h, or, m	0.0602	0.0688	0.0367	0.0695	0.0507	0.0680
nb, h, w, m	0.0162	0.0107	0.0177	0.0047	0.0242	0.0189
nb, h, aian, f	0.2111	0.2515	0.2848	0.3303	0.2793	0.1797
nb, h, api, f	0.1122	0.1498	0.1356	0.1929	0.1189	0.1729
nb, h, b, f	0.1041	0.1100	0.1831	0.2344	0.1684	0.2347
nb, h, mr, f	0.2165	0.1284	0.1933	0.2003	0.1977	0.1451
nb, h, or, f	0.1271	0.1720	0.1681	0.2289	0.2416	0.1886
nb, h, w, f	0.1474	0.1237	0.1533	0.2185	0.2295	0.0964
fb, nh, api, m	−0.1127	−0.1038	−0.1019	−0.1963	−0.1969	−0.1172

Panel A: Equation 3.9

Worker group	*2015*	*2016*	*2017*	*2018*	*2019*	*2020*
fb, nh, b, m	0.0753	0.0223	0.0430	0.0035	0.1552	0.0695
fb, nh, mr, m	−0.0134	−0.0154	0.0345	0.0195	−0.0281	−0.0392
fb, nh, or, m	−0.0054	0.1018	0.0828	0.0667	0.0426	0.0653
fb, nh, w, m	−0.1651	−0.1758	−0.1116	−0.2046	−0.2045	−0.1070
fb, nh, api, f	0.0385	0.0443	0.0270	0.0425	0.0124	0.0710
fb, nh, b, f	0.0459	0.1762	0.0821	0.1354	0.2591	0.1431
fb, nh, mr, f	0.1563	0.1455	0.1415	0.1662	0.2618	0.1496
fb, nh, or, f	0.1046	0.2011	0.1617	0.1773	0.1374	0.1956
fb, nh, w, f	0.0875	0.1140	0.0910	0.0655	0.1013	0.1730
fb, h, api, m	−0.0303	0.0275	.	0.1230	0.1087	0.0890
fb, h, b, m	0.1402	0.0737	−0.0018	0.1904	0.0848	0.1600
fb, h, mr, m	0.0834	0.0515	0.0631	0.0555	−0.0126	0.0014
fb, h, or, m	−0.0024	−0.0435	−0.0371	0.0170	−0.0426	−0.0899
fb, h, w, m	−0.0035	−0.0258	−0.0211	−0.0443	−0.0269	−0.0651
fb, h, api, f	.	0.2152	.	0.1811	.	0.1750
fb, h, b, f	0.2099	0.2248	0.2397	0.2827	0.2227	0.2491
fb, h, mr, f	0.1977	0.2690	0.1850	0.2171	0.2861	0.2097
fb, h, or, f	0.1291	0.1821	0.1661	0.1775	0.1997	0.1742
fb, h, w, f	0.2180	0.2176	0.1602	0.1712	0.2828	0.2095

(continued)

Table 4.4 (continued)

Panel B: Equation 3.10

Worker group	*2008*	*2009*	*2010*	*2011*	*2012*	*2013*	*2014*
nb, nh, aian, m	−0.0250	0.0462	−0.1492	0.0032	−0.0071	0.0251	−0.0118
nb, nh, api, m	0.0286	-0.0342	0.0161	−0.0027	−0.0022	0.0205	0.0295
nb, nh, b, m	0.0712	0.0587	0.0306	0.0601	0.0688	0.0577	0.0791
nb, nh, mr, m	0.0146	−0.0489	0.0035	−0.0016	−0.0108	−0.0196	−0.0088
nb, nh, or, m	0.1050	0.0641	0.1412	0.1274	0.0904	0.0904	0.0940
nb, nh, aian, f	0.1951	0.2164	0.1709	0.1057	0.1931	0.2080	0.2603
nb, nh, api, f	0.1162	0.1032	0.1006	0.1207	0.1096	0.1087	0.1085
nb, nh, b, f	0.1143	0.1418	0.1535	0.1545	0.1829	0.2115	0.1920
nb, nh, mr, f	0.2003	0.1101	0.1777	0.0949	0.1086	0.1822	0.1868
nb, nh, or, f	0.2014	0.1759	0.1621	0.0828	0.1881	0.1849	0.1639
nb, nh, w, f	0.1788	0.1656	0.1507	0.1460	0.1457	0.1568	0.1756
nb, h, aian, m	0.1198	0.1080	0.0859	0.0597	0.1473	0.1079	0.0662
nb, h, api, m	0.0391	0.1212	0.0330	0.0196	0.0141	0.0695	−0.0402
nb, h, b, m	0.0767	0.0763	0.0767	−0.0158	0.0939	0.0920	0.0695
nb, h, mr, m	0.0200	0.0347	0.0298	0.0428	0.0251	0.0343	0.0419
nb, h, or, m	0.0438	0.0318	0.0315	0.0566	0.0269	0.0756	0.0756
nb, h, w, m	0.0206	0.0153	−0.0112	0.0237	0.0187	0.0331	0.0104
nb, h, aian, f	0.2894	0.2628	0.2743	0.2012	0.2625	0.2154	0.1657
nb, h, api, f	0.1834	0.1406	0.0972	0.1723	0.1605	0.0762	0.1752
nb, h, b, f	0.1444	0.1643	0.1474	0.1688	0.1609	0.1690	0.2013

Panel B: Equation 3.10							
Worker group	*2008*	*2009*	*2010*	*2011*	*2012*	*2013*	*2014*
nb, h, mr, f	0.1505	0.1499	0.1939	0.1746	0.2133	0.1537	0.1561
nb, h, or, f	0.2105	0.1733	0.1877	0.1960	0.1827	0.2016	0.2085
nb, h, w, f	0.1698	0.1437	0.1482	0.1452	0.2079	0.1394	0.2010
fb, nh, api, m	−0.0096	−0.0229	0.0244	−0.0112	0.0020	−0.0183	−0.0018
fb, nh, b, m	0.0407	0.0618	0.0677	0.0841	0.2352	0.1037	0.0875
fb, nh, mr, m	0.1087	0.0475	0.0828	0.0588	0.0728	0.0525	0.0324
fb, nh, or, m	0.0871	0.1288	0.0202	0.1039	0.1176	0.0708	0.0102
fb, nh, w, m	−0.0979	−0.0775	−0.0553	−0.0947	−0.0761	−0.1532	−0.0923
fb, nh, api, f	0.1245	0.1406	0.1066	0.1252	0.0995	0.1192	0.1340
fb, nh, b, f	0.1724	0.1754	0.1097	0.2420	0.1944	0.1848	0.1384
fb, nh, mr, f	0.1649	0.1589	0.1807	0.1217	0.1728	0.2651	0.2388
fb, nh, or, f	0.2456	0.2262	0.1884	0.1961	0.1929	0.1936	0.1806
fb, nh, w, f	0.2023	0.1755	0.1234	0.1939	0.1145	0.1896	0.1711
fb, h, api, m	.	0.1051	0.0623	.	0.0899	0.1309	0.1692
fb, h, b, m	0.0596	0.1389	0.1560	0.1505	0.1537	0.1048	0.1935
fb, h, mr, m	0.1050	0.1090	0.0899	0.1547	0.1436	0.1606	0.1224
fb, h, or, m	0.1102	0.1066	0.0720	0.1103	0.1163	0.1382	0.0734
fb, h, w, m	0.0731	0.0504	0.0330	0.0990	0.1186	0.0820	0.0798
fb, h, api, f	0.1831	0.3460	0.1514	0.2308	.	.	0.2927
fb, h, b, f	0.2961	0.2147	0.2480	0.1997	0.2188	0.1829	0.2092
fb, h, mr, f	0.2753	0.2864	0.2700	0.2628	0.2500	0.2451	0.2859
fb, h, or, f	0.2805	0.2488	0.2484	0.1882	0.2682	0.2760	0.2742
fb, h, w, f	0.2070	0.2575	0.1987	0.2152	0.2604	0.2478	0.2717

(continued)

Table 4.4 (continued)

Panel B: Equation 3.10

Worker group	*2015*	*2016*	*2017*	*2018*	*2019*	*2020*
nb, nh, aian, m	0.0426	0.0243	0.0199	0.0358	0.0500	−0.0167
nb, nh, api, m	−0.0930	0.0106	−0.0117	−0.0256	−0.0203	−0.0510
nb, nh, b, m	0.0746	0.0746	0.0862	0.1038	0.1047	0.1035
nb, nh, mr, m	−0.0013	−0.0368	−0.0259	−0.0364	−0.0049	−0.0595
nb, nh, or, m	0.0417	0.0979	0.0941	0.0491	0.0740	0.0423
nb, nh, aian, f	0.1655	0.2452	0.1522	0.1427	0.2525	0.1716
nb, nh, api, f	0.1091	0.0758	0.0852	0.1300	0.1507	0.1383
nb, nh, b, f	0.1945	0.2184	0.2331	0.1949	0.2242	0.1594
nb, nh, mr, f	0.2076	0.1253	0.1489	0.1609	0.2142	0.1857
nb, nh, or, f	0.1786	0.1874	0.1995	0.1988	0.1757	0.1573
nb, nh, w, f	0.1670	0.1681	0.1639	0.1857	0.1759	0.1644
nb, h, aian, m	0.0422	0.1631	0.1267	0.1738	0.0926	0.0510
nb, h, api, m	0.0429	0.0883	0.0735	0.0590	0.0654	0.0389
nb, h, b, m	0.1167	0.1143	0.0693	0.1166	0.1152	0.0218
nb, h, mr, m	0.0462	0.0417	0.0080	0.0900	0.0514	0.0213
nb, h, or, m	0.0705	0.0676	0.0472	0.0709	0.0464	0.0766
nb, h, w, m	0.0238	0.0144	0.0224	0.0129	0.0200	0.0028
nb, h, aian, f	0.2054	0.2464	0.2604	0.3245	0.2681	0.1917
nb, h, api, f	0.1071	0.1570	0.1389	0.1903	0.1149	0.1637
nb, h, b, f	0.0977	0.1068	0.1534	0.2239	0.1520	0.2265
nb, h, mr, f	0.2137	0.1464	0.1945	0.1728	0.1869	0.1541
nb, h, or, f	0.1396	0.1564	0.1562	0.2116	0.2307	0.1979

Panel B: Equation 3.10

Worker group	*2015*	*2016*	*2017*	*2018*	*2019*	*2020*
nb, h, w, f	0.1741	0.1421	0.1830	0.2133	0.2227	0.1165
fb, nh, api, m	−0.0248	−0.0014	−0.0197	−0.0760	−0.0701	−0.0795
fb, nh, b, m	0.0849	0.0690	0.0624	0.0680	0.1511	0.1076
fb, nh, mr, m	0.0060	−0.0422	0.0311	0.0672	0.0154	−0.0345
fb, nh, or, m	0.0329	0.1302	0.1341	0.1032	0.0764	0.1043
fb, nh, w, m	−0.1182	−0.1378	−0.1113	−0.1498	−0.1390	−0.0588
fb, nh, api, f	0.1214	0.1066	0.1136	0.1291	0.1159	0.1170
fb, nh, b, f	0.1588	0.1954	0.1393	0.1846	0.2517	0.1945
fb, nh, mr, f	0.1875	0.1630	0.1458	0.1372	0.2448	0.1686
fb, nh, or, f	0.1222	0.2125	0.1752	0.1966	0.1610	0.2155
fb, nh, w, f	0.1366	0.1600	0.1075	0.0976	0.1770	0.1818
fb, h, api, m	0.0140	0.0663	.	0.1591	0.1486	0.1367
fb, h, b, m	0.1755	0.1113	0.0736	0.2143	0.1413	0.2024
fb, h, mr, m	0.1812	0.1265	0.1403	0.1403	0.0708	0.0735
fb, h, or, m	0.1140	0.0711	0.0827	0.1387	0.0729	0.0354
fb, h, w, m	0.0951	0.0763	0.0704	0.0689	0.0616	0.0235
fb, h, api, f	.	0.2258	.	0.1924	.	0.2295
fb, h, b, f	0.2149	0.2396	0.2515	0.2879	0.2369	0.2612
fb, h, mr, f	0.2600	0.3063	0.2309	0.2547	0.3088	0.2745
fb, h, or, f	0.1960	0.2451	0.2663	0.2867	0.2857	0.2368
fb, h, w, f	0.2960	0.2664	0.2477	0.2505	0.3296	0.2825

(continued)

Table 4.4 (continued)

Panel C: Equation 3.11

Worker group	*2008*	*2009*	*2010*	*2011*	*2012*	*2013*	*2014*
nb, nh, aian, m	−0.0321	0.0461	−0.1550	−0.0035	−0.0077	0.0258	−0.0124
nb, nh, api, m	0.0332	−0.0322	0.0104	−0.0008	0.0155	0.0299	0.0534
nb, nh, b, m	0.0729	0.0601	0.0298	0.0605	0.0685	0.0578	0.0780
nb, nh, mr, m	0.0150	−0.0489	0.0042	−0.0033	−0.0088	−0.0196	−0.0087
nb, nh, or, m	0.1034	0.0660	0.1406	0.1280	0.0887	0.0898	0.0938
nb, nh, aian, f	0.2352	0.2136	0.1727	0.0963	0.1846	0.2298	0.3312
nb, nh, api, f	0.1359	0.1016	0.1144	0.1280	0.1327	0.1210	0.1293
nb, nh, b, f	0.0644	0.0902	0.1149	0.1273	0.1588	0.1973	0.1676
nb, nh, mr, f	0.2105	0.1055	0.1640	0.0827	0.1084	0.1841	0.1847
nb, nh, or, f	0.2039	0.1797	0.1584	0.0837	0.1888	0.1802	0.1636
nb, nh, w, f	0.1954	0.1900	0.1660	0.1584	0.1636	0.1712	0.1975
nb, h, aian, m	0.1185	0.1065	0.0892	0.0577	0.1463	0.1068	0.0672
nb, h, api, m	0.0415	0.1264	0.0364	0.0204	0.0133	0.0704	−0.0404
nb, h, b, m	0.0761	0.0734	0.0737	−0.0137	0.0907	0.0915	0.0654
nb, h, mr, m	0.0189	0.0348	0.0285	0.0428	0.0215	0.0402	0.0414
nb, h, or, m	0.0421	0.0312	0.0309	0.0556	0.0270	0.0747	0.0747
nb, h, w, m	0.0198	0.0140	−0.0122	0.0231	0.0183	0.0317	0.0089
nb, h, aian, f	0.2862	0.2655	0.2752	0.2010	0.2620	0.2038	0.1706

Panel C: Equation 3.11

Worker group	*2008*	*2009*	*2010*	*2011*	*2012*	*2013*	*2014*
nb, h, api, f	0.1833	0.1282	0.0977	0.1731	0.1702	0.0758	0.1758
nb, h, b, f	0.1419	0.1651	0.1535	0.1710	0.1610	0.1715	0.2018
nb, h, mr, f	0.1558	0.1500	0.1951	0.1710	0.2195	0.1536	0.1531
nb, h, or, f	0.2141	0.1848	0.1906	0.1916	0.1823	0.2093	0.2005
nb, h, w, f	0.1724	0.1427	0.1487	0.1346	0.2364	0.1008	0.2055
fb, nh, api, m	−0.0257	−0.0460	0.0097	−0.0448	−0.0006	−0.0382	−0.0333
fb, nh, b, m	0.0313	0.0437	0.0648	0.0587	0.2808	0.1094	0.0877
fb, nh, mr, m	0.1115	0.0702	0.0812	0.0598	0.0760	0.0487	0.0323
fb, nh, or, m	0.0861	0.1291	0.0077	0.1056	0.1181	0.0709	0.0011
fb, nh, w, m	−0.0980	−0.0882	−0.0563	−0.0951	−0.0716	−0.1666	−0.1039
fb, nh, api, f	0.1276	0.1444	0.0962	0.1154	0.0777	0.0921	0.1386
fb, nh, b, f	0.1812	0.1566	0.0985	0.2536	0.2052	0.1783	0.1271
fb, nh, mr, f	0.1786	0.1616	0.1915	0.1340	0.1722	0.2761	0.2830
fb, nh, or, f	0.2426	0.2463	0.1905	0.1972	0.2143	0.1947	0.1802
fb, nh, w, f	0.2111	0.1824	0.1275	0.2140	0.1137	0.1883	0.1861
fb, h, api, m	.	0.1061	0.0531	.	0.0914	0.1197	0.1697
fb, h, b, m	0.0569	0.1379	0.1661	0.1515	0.1437	0.0899	0.1894
fb, h, mr, m	0.1062	0.1019	0.0898	0.1534	0.1447	0.1625	0.1200
fb, h, or, m	0.1117	0.1061	0.0716	0.1098	0.1187	0.1416	0.0736

(continued)

Table 4.4 (continued)

Panel C: Equation 3.11

Worker group	*2008*	*2009*	*2010*	*2011*	*2012*	*2013*	*2014*
fb, h, w, m	0.0710	0.0432	0.0311	0.0954	0.1170	0.0829	0.0584
fb, h, api, f	0.1884	0.3461	0.1495	0.2343	.	.	0.2932
fb, h, b, f	0.2984	0.2180	0.2505	0.2013	0.2192	0.1825	0.1999
fb, h, mr, f	0.2798	0.2857	0.2732	0.2629	0.2537	0.2561	0.2854
fb, h, or, f	0.2863	0.2500	0.2620	0.1892	0.2740	0.2802	0.2725
fb, h, w, f	0.1767	0.2462	0.1762	0.2028	0.2673	0.2277	0.2699

Panel C: Equation 3.11

Worker group	*2015*	*2016*	*2017*	*2018*	*2019*	*2020*
nb, nh, aian, m	0.0413	0.0290	0.0199	0.0359	0.0489	−0.0163
nb, nh, api, m	−0.1001	0.0055	−0.0507	−0.0418	−0.0237	−0.0510
nb, nh, b, m	0.0745	0.0736	0.0864	0.1030	0.1044	0.1025
nb, nh, mr, m	−0.0034	−0.0375	−0.0264	−0.0365	−0.0054	−0.0629
nb, nh, or, m	0.0295	0.0979	0.0921	0.0499	0.0713	0.0455
nb, nh, aian, f	0.1580	0.2478	0.1516	0.1592	0.2538	0.1699
nb, nh, api, f	0.1311	0.0745	0.0929	0.1517	0.1643	0.1527
nb, nh, b, f	0.1891	0.2115	0.2298	0.1715	0.1952	0.1432
nb, nh, mr, f	0.2327	0.1244	0.1538	0.1719	0.2292	0.1913
nb, nh, or, f	0.1813	0.1893	0.2006	0.1987	0.1757	0.1748
nb, nh, w, f	0.1802	0.1915	0.1855	0.2110	0.1941	0.1800
nb, h, aian, m	0.0418	0.1285	0.1249	0.1753	0.0928	0.0511

Panel C: Equation 3.11

Worker group	*2015*	*2016*	*2017*	*2018*	*2019*	*2020*
nb, h, api, m	0.0425	0.0865	0.0730	0.0590	0.0650	0.0399
nb, h, b, m	0.1176	0.1146	0.0702	0.1196	0.1201	0.0207
nb, h, mr, m	0.0480	0.0415	0.0084	0.0893	0.0514	0.0202
nb, h, or, m	0.0712	0.0680	0.0477	0.0709	0.0463	0.0767
nb, h, w, m	0.0228	0.0130	0.0222	0.0108	0.0178	0.0029
nb, h, aian, f	0.2053	0.2478	0.2726	0.3297	0.2646	0.1911
nb, h, api, f	0.1065	0.1565	0.1405	0.1901	0.1196	0.1630
nb, h, b, f	0.0975	0.1068	0.1533	0.2131	0.1454	0.2257
nb, h, mr, f	0.2213	0.1455	0.1923	0.1733	0.1834	0.1427
nb, h, or, f	0.1375	0.1557	0.1373	0.2107	0.2287	0.1947
nb, h, w, f	0.1624	0.1302	0.1791	0.2139	0.2227	0.0695
fb, nh, api, m	−0.0350	−0.0026	−0.0252	−0.0992	−0.0886	−0.0769
fb, nh, b, m	0.0881	0.0567	0.0628	0.0237	0.1520	0.1122
fb, nh, mr, m	0.0125	−0.0515	0.0706	0.0854	0.0142	−0.0356
fb, nh, or, m	0.0387	0.1308	0.1338	0.1031	0.0757	0.0968
fb, nh, w, m	−0.1283	−0.1488	−0.1185	−0.1542	−0.1912	−0.0478
fb, nh, api, f	0.1182	0.1100	0.1141	0.1344	0.1022	0.1190
fb, nh, b, f	0.0184	0.1954	0.1270	0.1764	0.2478	0.1306
fb, nh, mr, f	0.2255	0.1595	0.1381	0.1373	0.2446	0.1686
fb, nh, or, f	0.1220	0.2201	0.1845	0.1963	0.1613	0.2139

(continued)

Table 4.4 (continued)

Panel C: Equation 3.11

Worker group	*2015*	*2016*	*2017*	*2018*	*2019*	*2020*
fb, nh, w, f	0.1376	0.1720	0.1087	0.0934	0.1819	0.1874
fb, h, api, m	0.0136	0.0666	.	0.1470	0.1564	0.1464
fb, h, b, m	0.1826	0.1059	0.0762	0.2137	0.1425	0.2034
fb, h, mr, m	0.1782	0.1517	0.1399	0.1449	0.0732	0.0689
fb, h, or, m	0.1141	0.0707	0.0640	0.1424	0.0737	0.0364
fb, h, w, m	0.0935	0.0704	0.0654	0.0614	0.0638	0.0249
fb, h, api, f	.	0.2264	.	0.1948	.	0.2285
fb, h, b, f	0.2138	0.2385	0.2512	0.2907	0.2367	0.2614
fb, h, mr, f	0.2655	0.3230	0.2297	0.2549	0.3091	0.2749
fb, h, or, f	0.1952	0.2485	0.2996	0.2881	0.2860	0.2314
fb, h, w, f	0.3140	0.2652	0.2396	0.2542	0.3335	0.2800

Panel D: Equation 3.12

Worker group	*2008*	*2009*	*2010*	*2011*	*2012*	*2013*	*2014*
nb, nh, aian, m	−0.0202	0.0511	−0.0804	0.0075	−0.0079	0.0263	−0.0132
nb, nh, api, m	0.0244	−0.0350	0.0208	−0.0055	−0.0020	0.0237	0.0306
nb, nh, b, m	0.0749	0.0640	0.0331	0.0610	0.0696	0.0595	0.0795
nb, nh, mr, m	0.0164	−0.0420	0.0061	−0.0013	−0.0100	−0.0172	−0.0082
nb, nh, or, m	0.1050	0.0676	0.1366	0.1234	0.0871	0.0863	0.0918
nb, nh, aian, f	0.1902	0.2327	0.1591	0.1031	0.1905	0.1879	0.2195
nb, nh, api, f	0.1271	0.1132	0.1210	0.1297	0.1143	0.1150	0.1154

Panel D: Equation 3.12

Worker group	*2008*	*2009*	*2010*	*2011*	*2012*	*2013*	*2014*
nb, nh, b, f	0.1146	0.1343	0.1569	0.1590	0.1942	0.2102	0.1941
nb, nh, mr, f	0.1970	0.1137	0.1848	0.1270	0.1104	0.1602	0.1870
nb, nh, or, f	0.2057	0.1814	0.1762	0.0838	0.1917	0.1839	0.1712
nb, nh, w, f	0.1917	0.1817	0.1674	0.1649	0.1644	0.1710	0.1889
nb, h, aian, m	0.1310	0.1086	0.0942	0.0526	0.1357	0.1062	0.0658
nb, h, api, m	0.0397	0.1225	0.0403	0.0141	0.0156	0.0776	−0.0376
nb, h, b, m	0.0716	0.0779	0.0817	0.0625	0.0885	0.0830	0.0650
nb, h, mr, m	0.0329	0.0376	0.0288	0.0418	0.0215	0.0359	0.0539
nb, h, or, m	0.0434	0.0304	0.0308	0.0547	0.0245	0.0721	0.0725
nb, h, w, m	0.0213	0.0123	−0.0122	0.0222	0.0162	0.0323	0.0085
nb, h, aian, f	0.2881	0.2683	0.2774	0.1967	0.2643	0.2039	0.1648
nb, h, api, f	0.1897	0.1461	0.0992	0.1743	0.1692	0.0855	0.1777
nb, h, b, f	0.1449	0.1696	0.1567	0.1717	0.1653	0.1713	0.1990
nb, h, mr, f	0.1642	0.1570	0.1901	0.1859	0.2164	0.1503	0.1576
nb, h, or, f	0.2156	0.1735	0.1767	0.1883	0.1835	0.2008	0.2110
nb, h, w, f	0.1730	0.1530	0.1597	0.1590	0.2138	0.1467	0.2086
fb, nh, api, m	−0.0213	−0.0334	0.0138	−0.0301	−0.0129	−0.0304	−0.0179
fb, nh, b, m	0.0329	0.0602	0.0693	0.0868	0.2203	0.1043	0.0862
fb, nh, mr, m	0.1041	0.0437	0.0855	0.0506	0.0615	0.0410	0.0290
fb, nh, or, m	0.0918	0.1480	0.0220	0.1099	0.1214	0.0702	0.0299

(continued)

Table 4.4 (continued)

Panel D: Equation 3.12

Worker group	*2008*	*2009*	*2010*	*2011*	*2012*	*2013*	*2014*
fb, nh, w, m	−0.1086	−0.0863	−0.0740	−0.1168	−0.0956	−0.1747	−0.1081
fb, nh, api, f	0.1246	0.1345	0.1119	0.1254	0.1022	0.1195	0.1333
fb, nh, b, f	0.1723	0.1853	0.1097	0.2276	0.1910	0.1932	0.1427
fb, nh, mr, f	0.1657	0.1657	0.1900	0.1304	0.1733	0.2940	0.2310
fb, nh, or, f	0.2443	0.2336	0.1860	0.1959	0.2067	0.1999	0.1923
fb, nh, w, f	0.1972	0.1639	0.1197	0.1845	0.1067	0.1700	0.1714
fb, h, api, m	.	0.1229	0.0734	.	0.1223	0.1686	0.1748
fb, h, b, m	0.0750	0.1630	0.1771	0.1692	0.1710	0.1057	0.2002
fb, h, mr, m	0.1292	0.1352	0.1329	0.1796	0.1774	0.1813	0.1478
fb, h, or, m	0.1385	0.1391	0.1165	0.1465	0.1440	0.1600	0.1018
fb, h, w, m	0.0997	0.0768	0.0645	0.1295	0.1425	0.1024	0.1049
fb, h, api, f	0.1952	0.3578	0.1750	0.2459	.	.	0.3102
fb, h, b, f	0.3124	0.2260	0.2613	0.2117	0.2317	0.1906	0.2148
fb, h, mr, f	0.2882	0.3043	0.2991	0.2744	0.2596	0.2597	0.3000
fb, h, or, f	0.2973	0.2638	0.2732	0.2256	0.2873	0.2961	0.2962
fb, h, w, f	0.2223	0.2726	0.2191	0.2367	0.2823	0.2632	0.2891

Panel D: Equation 3.12

Worker group	*2015*	*2016*	*2017*	*2018*	*2019*	*2020*
nb, nh, aian, m	0.0421	0.0225	0.0190	0.0367	0.0460	−0.0144
nb, nh, api, m	−0.0921	0.0061	−0.0090	−0.0305	−0.0293	−0.0445

Panel D: Equation 3.12

Worker group	*2015*	*2016*	*2017*	*2018*	*2019*	*2020*
nb, nh, b, m	0.0738	0.0769	0.0870	0.1043	0.1046	0.1118
nb, nh, mr, m	−0.0041	−0.0318	−0.0217	−0.0334	−0.0027	−0.0572
nb, nh, or, m	0.0428	0.0995	0.1046	0.0548	0.0769	0.0383
nb, nh, aian, f	0.1648	0.2262	0.1470	0.1421	0.2463	0.1791
nb, nh, api, f	0.1091	0.0682	0.0769	0.1213	0.1381	0.1302
nb, nh, b, f	0.2001	0.2123	0.2359	0.1976	0.2196	0.1931
nb, nh, mr, f	0.1984	0.1247	0.1497	0.1633	0.2115	0.1830
nb, nh, or, f	0.1824	0.2043	0.2097	0.2027	0.1773	0.1562
nb, nh, w, f	0.1790	0.1809	0.1749	0.1948	0.1838	0.1649
nb, h, aian, m	0.0401	0.1699	0.1209	0.1564	0.0991	0.0459
nb, h, api, m	0.0455	0.0873	0.0785	0.0585	0.0590	0.0410
nb, h, b, m	0.1092	0.1120	0.0725	0.1122	0.1194	0.0208
nb, h, mr, m	0.0448	0.0397	0.0078	0.0893	0.0513	0.0212
nb, h, or, m	0.0666	0.0652	0.0437	0.0655	0.0456	0.0752
nb, h, w, m	0.0217	0.0117	0.0199	0.0102	0.0191	0.0076
nb, h, aian, f	0.2078	0.2514	0.2599	0.3325	0.2670	0.1948
nb, h, api, f	0.1156	0.1606	0.1477	0.1917	0.1241	0.1745
nb, h, b, f	0.1062	0.1078	0.1548	0.2236	0.1597	0.2330
nb, h, mr, f	0.2219	0.1561	0.1895	0.1596	0.1856	0.1549
nb, h, or, f	0.1404	0.1577	0.1552	0.2078	0.2316	0.1998

(continued)

Table 4.4 (continued)

Panel D: Equation 3.12

Worker group	*2015*	*2016*	*2017*	*2018*	*2019*	*2020*
nb, h, w, f	0.1843	0.1515	0.1859	0.2152	0.2213	0.1192
fb, nh, api, m	−0.0416	−0.0116	−0.0331	−0.0885	−0.0796	−0.0893
fb, nh, b, m	0.0840	0.0676	0.0576	0.0897	0.1577	0.1090
fb, nh, mr, m	−0.0017	0.0031	0.0265	0.0633	0.0088	−0.0360
fb, nh, or, m	0.0277	0.1267	0.1431	0.1158	0.0756	0.1082
fb, nh, w, m	−0.1395	−0.1655	−0.1325	−0.1736	−0.1646	−0.0841
fb, nh, api, f	0.1245	0.1082	0.1096	0.1262	0.1142	0.1115
fb, nh, b, f	0.1772	0.1999	0.1549	0.1977	0.2530	0.1937
fb, nh, mr, f	0.1847	0.1634	0.1480	0.1374	0.2299	0.1694
fb, nh, or, f	0.1303	0.2102	0.1838	0.2037	0.1737	0.2167
fb, nh, w, f	0.1189	0.1468	0.0930	0.0711	0.1578	0.1569
fb, h, api, m	0.0211	0.0779	0.0894	0.1665	0.1524	0.1509
fb, h, b, m	0.1892	0.1172	0.0894	0.2175	0.1533	0.2094
fb, h, mr, m	0.2052	0.1551	0.1605	0.1570	0.0794	0.0946
fb, h, or, m	0.1398	0.1010	0.1366	0.1727	0.1061	0.0729
fb, h, w, m	0.1190	0.1018	0.0930	0.0930	0.0843	0.0449
fb, h, api, f	.	0.2396	.	0.2095	.	0.2327
fb, h, b, f	0.2174	0.2469	0.2584	0.2969	0.2332	0.2734
fb, h, mr, f	0.2680	0.3139	0.2427	0.2665	0.3147	0.2881
fb, h, or, f	0.2097	0.2634	0.2917	0.3076	0.3014	0.2623
fb, h, w, f	0.3024	0.2822	0.2613	0.2659	0.3410	0.2968

Note See Appendix Table 4.2 notes

CHAPTER 5

Evidence of Intersectional Wage Discrimination and an Examination of Possible Pre-market Discrimination

Abstract To determine whether wage discrimination in the U.S. labor market is intersectional, we compare estimated discrimination rates to expected discrimination rates. For a given worker group, its expected discrimination rate is the sum of personal characteristic-specific discrimination rates. These characteristic-specific discrimination rates are obtained by comparing each worker group that differs from our null worker cohort of native-born, non-Hispanic, white, male workers in two or more personal characteristics to another worker group that differs by a single characteristic. This involves the application of the Blinder-Oaxaca decomposition technique with a Heckman sample selection correction model to the Mincer earnings function. If for a given worker group, the expected discrimination rate is within five percentage points of the estimated discrimination rate, we conclude that wage discrimination is additive. If, however, the difference between estimated and expected discrimination rates is more than five percentage points, then we conclude that the wage discrimination is intersectional (i.e., non-additive). As a modest application of our findings, we consider a possible statistical relationship between pre-labor market discrimination and intersectional wage discrimination.

Keywords Additive assumption · Expected wage discrimination · Intersectional wage discrimination · Pre-market discrimination · Returns to schooling

R. White, *Intersectionality and Discrimination*,
https://doi.org/10.1007/978-3-031-26125-1_5

In Chapter 4, we documented considerable variation in estimated wage discrimination rates across the 43 worker groups that we compare to our null worker cohort. In this chapter, we build on those results by addressing our primary research question: Is wage discrimination intersectional? We also extend from the findings reported in Chapter 4 to consider possible pre-labor market discrimination by examining variation in returns to education across worker groups. We do this by examining differences in returns to schooling and by evaluating the relationships between average estimated discrimination rates and returns to schooling across levels of educational attainment.

As a preview of our findings, we can state that, with respect to the question of additive or non-additive discrimination, we present evidence that strongly suggests wage discrimination is frequently, although not exclusively, non-additive (i.e., intersectional). With regard to pre-labor market discrimination, while our estimated returns to education are consistent with pre-market discrimination, we do not find evidence to support a statistical relationship between intersectional wage discrimination and pre-labor market discrimination related to education.

5.1 Evidence of Intersectional Wage Discrimination

We begin with some preliminaries. First, discrimination is said to be additive when an individual suffers discrimination that is simultaneous and related to multiple personal characteristics. For example, if a native-born, non-Hispanic, black, female worker simultaneously faces discrimination due to her race and her sex, then the discrimination suffered is additive because the two personal characteristics are independent. This differs from sequential multiple discrimination which occurs when an individual suffers discrimination related to multiple characteristics at different moments in time. Second, intersectional discrimination is similar to additive discrimination in that it involves simultaneous discrimination that is related to multiple characteristics; however, it is non-additive. This means the multiple personal characteristics interact in a manner that produces a unique form of discrimination that is specific to the individual's intersecting identities.

An example may help differentiate between additive discrimination and intersectional discrimination. Assume a worker who is native-born, Hispanic, white, and female suffers wage discrimination because of her sex and because of her Hispanic ethnicity. Further assume that, compared to an equally productive native-born, Hispanic, white, male worker, this individual is paid some amount (d) less due to sex-based discrimination and an additional amount (a) less due to ethnicity-based discrimination. Thus, she simultaneously suffers discrimination related to two personal characteristics. If the difference between this worker's wage and the wage of their equally productive native-born, non-Hispanic, white, male counterpart (i.e., the unexplained portion of the wage gap (f)) is equal to the sum of the individual discrimination estimates (i.e., if $a + d = f$), then the discrimination is additive. If, however, $a + d \neq f$, then it follows that this worker's particular combination of identities creates a unique and distinct form of discrimination that is intersectional (i.e., non-additive) (g) such that $a + d + g = f$, with g being non-zero (i.e., either positive or negative). As is evident, this example can be extended to additional differences in identities/personal characteristics.

To explore whether the estimated discrimination rates presented in Chapter 4 are additive or intersectional, we consider whether the unexplained wage gaps that are attributed to discrimination (i.e., estimated discrimination rates) differ from the sum of characteristic-specific discriminations (i.e., expected discrimination rates). This is the same general process employed by Kim (2009), Paul et al. (2022), and George et al. (2022). While the estimated discrimination rates were obtained by comparing each of the worker groups, in turn, to our null worker cohort, the expected discrimination rates are calculated by estimating personal characteristic-specific discrimination rates for each worker group. We then sum the resulting values to obtain our expected discrimination rates and then compare the expected discrimination rates to the estimated discrimination rates. If for a given worker group, the expected rate and estimated rate are within five percentage points (i.e., if the values are approximately equal), then we conclude that the wage discrimination is additive. If, however, the values are not approximately equal, then we identify the discrimination as intersectional.

We estimate characteristic-specific discrimination rates by comparing a given worker group to another worker group that differs only by the single characteristic that is being considered. This produces an estimate of discrimination that is related to the specific characteristic that differentiates the two groups. In each instance, we estimate two Mincer earnings functions (i.e., Eqs. 3.9 and 3.12) again using the Blinder-Oaxaca decomposition technique while employing the Heckman sample selection model. We repeat this process until all differences in personal characteristics between the specific worker group and the null worker cohort have been considered.

An additional example of the process may help to explain. Given the native-born, non-Hispanic, black, female worker group differs from our null cohort of native-born, non-Hispanic, white, male workers in terms of race and sex (i.e., c and d), and we have the estimated discrimination rate (f) from our analysis that is presented in Chapter 4, to determine if the discrimination suffered by members of this worker group is additive or intersectional we must obtain separate discrimination rate estimates for race (c) and sex (d), sum the values to produce the expected discrimination rate (e), and compare the resulting value to our estimated discrimination rate. To discern the race-based discrimination rate for native-born, non-Hispanic, black, female workers, we compare the group to the native-born, non-Hispanic, white, female worker group. Note that, across the four personal characteristics that we consider, these two groups differ only in terms of race. Similarly, to estimate the sex-based discrimination rate, we compare the native-born, non-Hispanic, black, female worker group to the native-born, non-Hispanic, black, male worker group. Here, again in terms of characteristics considered, sex is the only difference between the two worker groups.

Results obtained when estimating Eq. 3.9 while using data for the year 2020 are presented in Table 5.1. Corresponding results from the estimation of Eq. 3.12 are provided in Table 5.2. The estimates of race-based discrimination for the native-born, non-Hispanic, black, female worker group are equal to 5.95% (from Eq. 3.9) and 0.97% (from Eq. 3.12). The estimates of sex-based discrimination for this group are 6.17% (from Eq. 3.9) and 1.34% (from Eq. 3.12). These values are reported in columns (c) and (d) of the tables.[1] The sums of the characteristic-specific discrimination rates are presented in column (e) and are referred to as our expected discrimination rates. For our example worker group, the expected discrimination rates are 12.12% (Eq. 3.9) and 2.31% (Eq. 3.12).

[1] The characteristic-specific discrimination rates for nativity and Hispanic ethnicity are presented in columns (a) and (b), respectively. Since native-born, non-Hispanic, black female workers do not differ from the null worker cohort in terms of nativity or Hispanic ethnicity, “n.a.” is reported in each table.

The corresponding estimated discrimination rates are presented in column (f) of each table.[2]

Beginning with the values presented for the native-born, non-Hispanic, black, female worker group in Table 5.1, since the estimated discrimination rate is equal to 24.85% and the expected discrimination rate is 12.12%, we have evidence in support of intersectional wage discrimination. (i.e., $c + d \neq f$; thus, $g \neq 0$). This suggests that the particular combination of personal characteristics of the native-born, non-Hispanic, black, female worker group interacts to create a unique and distinct form of discrimination. Specifically, the intersectional discrimination estimate (g) is estimated to equal 12.73% (i.e., $g = f - c - d$). The corresponding values that are presented in Table 5.2 again support the presence of intersectional wage discrimination for this worker group. Here, the expected discrimination rate is equal to 2.31%, while the estimated discrimination rate is 19.31%; thus, the intersectional discrimination estimate is 17.0%. Our finding of intersectional wage discrimination (i.e., non-additive discrimination) against native-born, non-Hispanic, black, female workers is somewhat consistent with the results presented in Paul et al. (2022) and George et al. (2022). The finding is also somewhat consistent with the results obtained by Kim (2009) when she did not include controls for each worker's industry of employment and occupation classification in her estimation equation.[3]

We perform this same estimation process for each of the worker groups for which statistically significant estimated discrimination rates are presented in panels A and D of Table 4.2. This results in the examination of whether discrimination is intersectional for 22 worker groups (Eq. 3.9) and 25 groups (Eq. 3.12). In both instances, we find evidence in support of intersectional wage discrimination for the majority of worker groups considered. Specifically, in Table 5.1, we see that the absolute value of g is greater than five percentage points for 13 of the 22 worker groups (59.1%). Similarly, in Table 5.2, $|g| > 0.05$ for 16 of 25 worker groups (64%). Admittedly, five percentage points is an arbitrary threshold;

[2] The values in column (f) of Table 5.1 and Table 5.2 are also presented in the rightmost columns of panels A and D of Appendix Table 4.4.

[3] Our results are not entirely comparable to the findings reported in earlier studies since Kim (2009), Paul et al. (2022), and George et al. (2022) all examine black female workers (without considering the characteristics of nativity and Hispanic ethnicity) while we examine native-born, non-Hispanic, black, female workers.

Table 5.1 Expected discrimination rates, characteristic-specific contributions, and estimated discrimination rates, 2020 (Eq. 3.9)

						Discrimination		
		Ethnicity	*Nativity*	*Race*	*Sex*	*Expected*	*Estimated*	*Dif.: (f)-(e)*
Group	*N Dif.*	*(a)*	*(b)*	*(c)*	*(d)*	*(e)*	*(f)*	*(g)*
fb, nh, b, f	3	n.a.	−0.0963	−0.0109	−0.0397	−0.1469	0.1431*	0.2900
nb, h, aian, f	3	−0.0335	n.a.	−0.0203	0.0267	−0.0271	0.1797***	0.2068
nb, h, mr, f	3	−0.0348	n.a.	−0.0579*	0.0627*	−0.0300	0.1451***	0.1751
nb, nh, b, f	2	n.a.	n.a.	0.0595***	0.0617***	0.1212	0.2485***	0.1273
nb, h, mr, m	2	−0.0226*	n.a.	−0.0600***	n.a.	−0.0825	0.0249**	0.1074
fb, h, or, f	4	−0.0024	0.0038	−0.0085	0.0793**	0.0721	0.1742***	0.1021
nb, nh, or, f	2	n.a.	n.a.	−0.0186	0.0620	0.0434	0.1451***	0.1017
nb, nh, aian, f	2	n.a.	n.a.	0.0328**	0.1011***	0.1340	0.2217***	0.0877
fb, nh, mr, f	3	n.a.	−0.0438	0.0023	0.1279**	0.0864	0.1496***	0.0632
fb, h, api, f	4	0.0272	0.0609	−0.0810*	0.1148	0.1219	0.175***	0.0531
nb, h, or, f	3	0.0767***	n.a.	0.0046	0.0706***	0.1519	0.1886***	0.0367

						Discrimination		
		Ethnicity	*Nativity*	*Race*	*Sex*	*Expected*	*Estimated*	*Dif.: (f)-(e)*
Group	*N Dif.*	*(a)*	*(b)*	*(c)*	*(d)*	*(e)*	*(f)*	*(g)*
fb, h, mr, f	4	0.0777*	0.0166	−0.0328	0.1219***	0.1833	0.2097***	0.0264
nb, h, or, m	2	0.0464*	n.a.	0.0063	n.a.	0.0527	0.068***	0.0153
nb, nh, mr, f	2	n.a.	n.a.	0.0411***	0.1483***	0.1894	0.2015***	0.0121
fb, nh, api, m	2	n.a.	−0.0936	−0.0356	n.a.	−0.1292	−0.1172*	0.0120
fb, nh, or, f	3	n.a.	0.0138	0.0566	0.1264*	0.1967	0.1956***	−0.0011
nb, h, b, f	3	0.0443	n.a.	0.0902**	0.1205**	0.2550	0.2347***	−0.0203
fb, h, w, f	3	0.0564***	0.0073	n.a.	0.1677***	0.2314	0.2095***	−0.0219
nb, h, api, f	3	0.0997*	n.a.	−0.0185	0.1314*	0.2126	0.1729***	−0.0397
fb, nh, w, f	2	n.a.	0.0057	n.a.	0.2466***	0.2523	0.173***	−0.0793
fb, h, b, m	3	0.0452	0.0990*	0.1116***	n.a.	0.2558	0.16***	−0.0958
fb, h, api, m	3	0.0930**	0.1534*	−0.0183	n.a.	0.2281	0.089**	−0.1391

Note "***", "**", and "*" denote statistical significance from zero at the 1%, 5%, and 10% levels, respectively. Entries of "n.a." indicate that the corresponding characteristic does not differ from the null worker cohort. fb = foreign-born, nb = native-born, h = Hispanic, nh = non-Hispanic, aian = American Indian and Alaska native, api = Asian or Pacific Islander, b = black, mr = multiple races, or = other race, w = white, f = female, and m = male

Table 5.2 Expected discrimination rates, characteristic-specific contributions, and estimated discrimination rates, 2020 (Eq. 3.12)

						Discrimination		
		Ethnicity	*Nativity*	*Race*	*Sex*	*Expected*	*Estimated*	*Dif.: (f)−(e)*
Group	*N Dif.*	*(a)*	*(b)*	*(c)*	*(d)*	*(e)*	*(f)*	*(g)*
fb, nh, b, f	3	n.a.	−0.0454	0.0225	−0.0099	−0.0329	0.1937***	0.2266
nb, h, aian, f	3	−0.0193	n.a.	−0.0068	0.0489*	0.0228	0.1948***	0.1720
nb, nh, b, f	2	n.a.	n.a.	0.0097	0.0134	0.0231	0.1931***	0.1700
nb, h, mr, f	3	−0.0193	n.a.	−0.0456*	0.0724***	0.0071	0.1549***	0.1478
fb, h, or, f	4	0.0228	0.0342	−0.0066	0.0868**	0.1373	0.2623***	0.1250
nb, nh, aian, f	2	n.a.	n.a.	−0.0031	0.0713***	0.0681	0.1791***	0.1110
nb, h, w, f	2	−0.0271	n.a.	n.a.	0.0358	0.0087	0.1192*	0.1105
fb, h, mr, m	3	0.0410	0.0058	−0.0557*	n.a.	−0.0089	0.0946***	0.1035
nb, nh, or, f	2	n.a.	n.a.	−0.0062	0.0607	0.0545	0.1562***	0.1017
fb, h, api, f	4	0.0159	0.1314	−0.0666	0.0959	0.1766	0.2327***	0.0561
fb, nh, mr, f	3	n.a.	−0.0209	0.0096	0.1268***	0.1156	0.1694***	0.0538

Group	N Dif.	Ethnicity	Nativity	Race	Sex	Discrimination		
						Expected	Estimated	Dif.: (f)−(e)
		(a)	(b)	(c)	(d)	(e)	(f)	(g)
nb, h, or, m	2	0.0325	n.a.	−0.0025	n.a.	0.0300	0.0752***	0.0452
fb, nh, api, f	3	n.a.	0.0357	−0.0547	0.0867**	0.0677	0.1115***	0.0438
nb, h, or, f	3	0.0646**	n.a.	0.0122	0.0795***	0.1564	0.1998***	0.0434
nb, nh, mr, f	2	n.a.	n.a.	0.0234**	0.1317***	0.1551	0.183***	0.0279
fb, nh, or, f	3	n.a.	0.0290	0.0638	0.1064	0.1992	0.2167***	0.0175
nb, nh, api, f	2	n.a.	n.a.	0.0083	0.1373***	0.1456	0.1302***	−0.0154
nb, h, b, f	3	0.0433	n.a.	0.0894***	0.1204**	0.2531	0.233***	−0.0201
nb, h, api, f	3	0.0773	n.a.	−0.0223	0.1528**	0.2077	0.1745***	−0.0332
fb, h, b, m	3	0.0454	0.1153**	0.0946**	n.a.	0.2553	0.2094***	−0.0459
fb, nh, w, f	2	n.a.	−0.0135	n.a.	0.2240***	0.2105	0.1569***	−0.0536
fb, h, mr, f	4	0.1151***	0.0855***	0.0080	0.1455***	0.3541	0.2881***	−0.0660
fb, h, w, f	3	0.1197***	0.0770***	n.a.	0.1887***	0.3855	0.2968***	−0.0887
fb, nh, or, m	2	n.a.	0.0497	0.1525***	n.a.	0.2022	0.1082*	−0.0940
fb, h, api, m	3	0.0834**	0.1703**	0.0229	n.a.	0.2766	0.1509***	−0.1257

Note See Table 5.1 notes

however, a higher threshold value—say, one equal to 0.10—would still suggest intersectional wage discrimination for eight of the worker groups listed in Table 5.1 and 10 of the worker groups included in Table 5.2.

Across the two tables, we see considerable overlap in terms of the worker groups for which there is evidence of intersectional discrimination. In total, 26 worker groups are represented in one or both tables. By this metric, we find evidence of intersectional discrimination for at least 18 of these groups. Outside of the great frequency at which these 18 groups include female workers (i.e., 13 of the 18 groups include female workers), there is great diversity in terms of Hispanic ethnicity, nativity, and race across the worker groups. When this diversity is considered with the knowledge that the estimated discrimination rates are statistically significant from zero, we must conclude that intersectional wage discrimination appears to occur more often than additive wage discrimination and that the personal characteristics considered do appear to combine to create unique and distinct forms of discrimination.

Lastly, similar to the findings reported in Paul et al. (2022), we do not find common levels of Hispanic ethnicity-, nativity-, race-, or sex-based discrimination across the worker groups considered. In Table 5.2, the magnitudes of statistically significant ethnicity-based discrimination rates vary from 6.46% for the native-born, Hispanic, other race, female worker group to 11.97% for the foreign-born, Hispanic, white, female group. With respect to nativity, statistically significant discrimination rates range from 7.7% for the foreign-born, Hispanic, white, female group to 17.03% for the foreign-born, Hispanic, Asian or Pacific Islander, male worker group. Similarly, statistically significant race-based discrimination rates vary from a low of −5.57% for the foreign-born, Hispanic, multiple race, male worker group to a high of 15.25% for foreign-born, non-Hispanic, other race, males. Lastly, estimates of sex-based discrimination range from 4.89% for the native-born, Hispanic, American Indian and Alaska native, female worker group to 22.4% for foreign-born, non-Hispanic, white, female workers.

5.2 Examining Possible Pre-market Discrimination

In simple terms, pre-market discrimination is discrimination that a worker experiences before entering the labor market. There are various forms of pre-market discrimination. For example, pre-market discrimination occurs if a worker is disadvantaged due to their parents having low levels of educational attainment due to discrimination. Similarly, a worker suffers pre-market discrimination if they completed their education in a school system characterized by discrimination-related inequities. A third example holds that a worker suffers pre-market discrimination if, as a consequence of discrimination, they were raised in an impoverished neighborhood. These examples involve discrimination in education and housing but there are myriad ways in which an individual's labor market outcomes may be affected by discrimination that is suffered before entering the labor market.

In this section, we close our analysis with an examination of the estimated returns to education that were obtained when we generated our estimated discrimination rates. Specifically, we focus on the information obtained from the estimations of Eqs. (3.9) and (3.12). Thus, we have estimates, for each of our worker groups and for our null worker cohort, of the effect that an additional year of schooling has on the hourly wage rate. Similarly, we have estimates of the returns to earning a high school diploma or equivalent degree, completing some college coursework, earning a four-year degree, and undertaking graduate study. Finally, once we have presented our estimates, we compare the average estimated discrimination rates for each worker group to the corresponding average returns to education for each educational attainment classification that are estimated from annual values over the 2008–2020 period.

Figure 5.1 illustrates the average, minimum, and maximum coefficient estimates for our null worker cohort and each of the 43 comparison worker groups.[4] The average values are calculated as the simple mean across each worker group's 13-year-specific estimates that were obtained via the estimation of Eq. 3.9. The values in the figure are presented in ascending order from left to right with the corresponding worker group identified on the x-axis. For additional reference, we identify the mean value (0.0532) across the worker groups. Given the functional form of equation (3.9) and that the corresponding education variable is measured in years of schooling completed, we can interpret this value as follows: If the typical worker completes an additional year of schooling, all else held constant, the hourly wage rate would increase by 5.32%.

[4] The year-specific estimates of returns to years of schooling are provided for each worker group in Appendix Table 5.3.

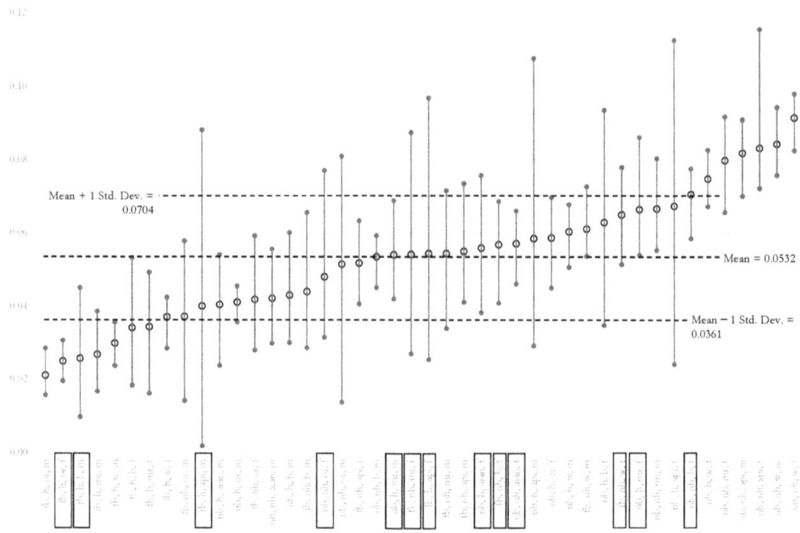

Fig. 5.1 Estimated returns to education (measured in years)—average, minimum, and maximum coefficient values, 2008-2020 (*Note* Presented coefficient values correspond to estimation of Eq. 3.9. Values are unweighted means. See Table 5.1 notes for an explanation of abbreviations)

It is important to note that the estimated returns to education—whether measured in years or by the level of educational attainment—are relative to a worker from the same group who, in the case of returns to years of schooling, has completed no formal education or, in the case of returns to educational attainment, has not completed a high school diploma or equivalent credential. Thus, our discussion in this section is predicated on the assumption that there are no significant differences across worker groups in the returns to education of workers with no formal schooling (Eq. 3.9) or in the returns to education of workers who have not completed high school (Eq. 3.12). We proceed cautiously with this assumption in mind.

In Fig. 5.1, we also identify the range from one standard deviation below the mean value (0.0361) to one standard deviation above the mean (0.0704). Of note is that the average return to education for the null worker cohort of native-born, non-Hispanic, white, males (0.0843) is second highest to the native-born, non-Hispanic, white, female worker group (0.0915). At the other end of the figure, the two groups with the lowest average returns to education include foreign-born, Hispanic, other race, male workers (0.0211) and foreign-born, Hispanic, other race, female workers (0.0249).

We find no clear evidence of a relationship between intersectional wage discrimination and pre-market discrimination that manifests through lower returns to years of schooling. In Fig. 5.1, on the x-axis, boxes have been placed around the labels for each of the 13 worker groups that are reported in Table 5.1 to experience intersectional wage discrimination. A cursory review of the figure reveals no discernible pattern between the two series. In fact, nine of the 13 worker groups identified as experiencing intersectional wage discrimination have above-average values for returns to years of schooling. Further, the mean value for returns to years of schooling for the group that experiences intersectional wage discrimination is equal to 0.0554 (i.e., 5.54%), while the corresponding mean value for the remaining 31 worker groups is nearly identical at 0.0551 (i.e., 5.51%).

We include four panels in Fig. 5.2. Each panel illustrates the returns to a different level of educational attainment for all worker groups.[5] For example, panel A illustrates the returns to the completion of high school, panel B illustrates the returns to the completion of some college coursework, etc. In each panel, we present the mean returns to educational attainment that are calculated across all worker groups. We also identify our null worker cohort which is the highest or second-highest value in each panel. Given the functional form of Eq. 3.12 and that educational attainment is measured in categories, the values are to be interpreted relative to the excluded educational attainment category of less than a high school diploma (or the equivalent). Thus, the mean return of high school completion across all worker groups is an hourly wage that is 5.18% higher than that of a comparable worker who did not complete high school. The average return to the completion of some college coursework is a 14% higher hourly wage than a comparable worker who lacks a high school education. Similarly, the average returns to four-year college graduates and those who complete some graduate coursework are hourly wage rates that are 36.07% and 57.65% higher, respectively, than the rate paid to workers who have not completed high school.

[5] The year-specific returns to levels of educational attainment are provided for each worker group in Appendix Table 5.4.

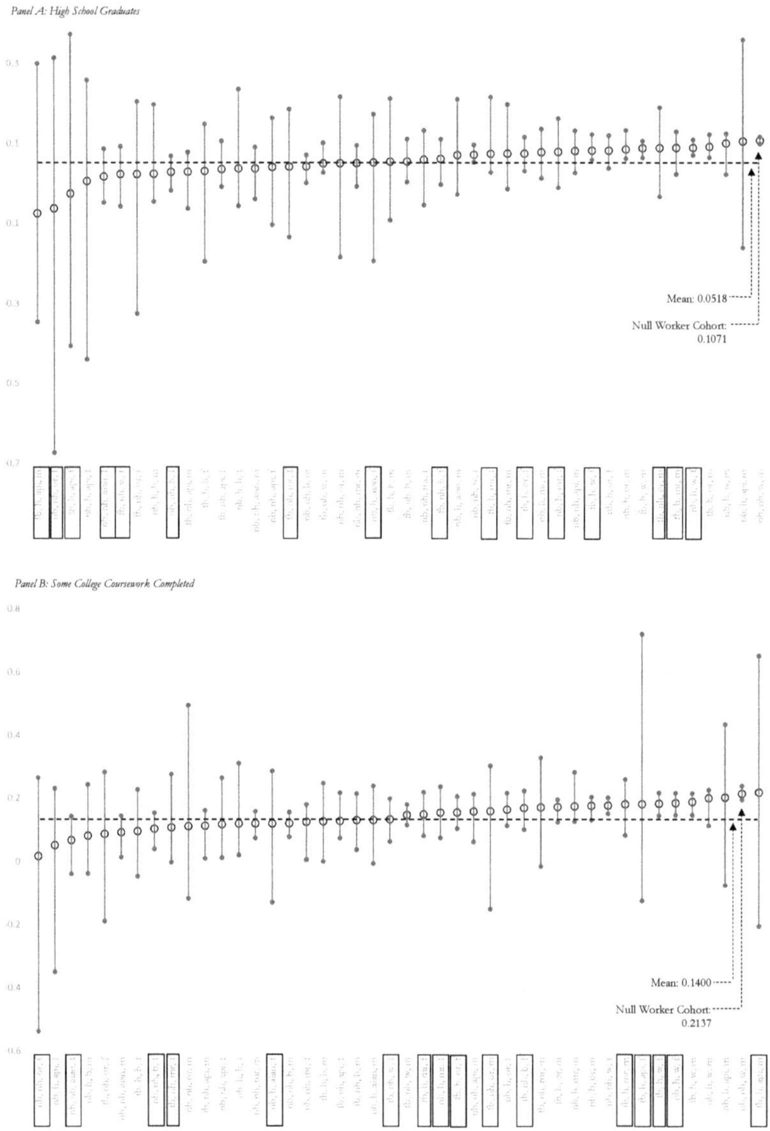

Fig. 5.2 Estimated returns to education (by level of educational attainment)—average, minimum, and maximum coefficient values, 2008–2020 (*Notes* See Fig. 5.1 notes)

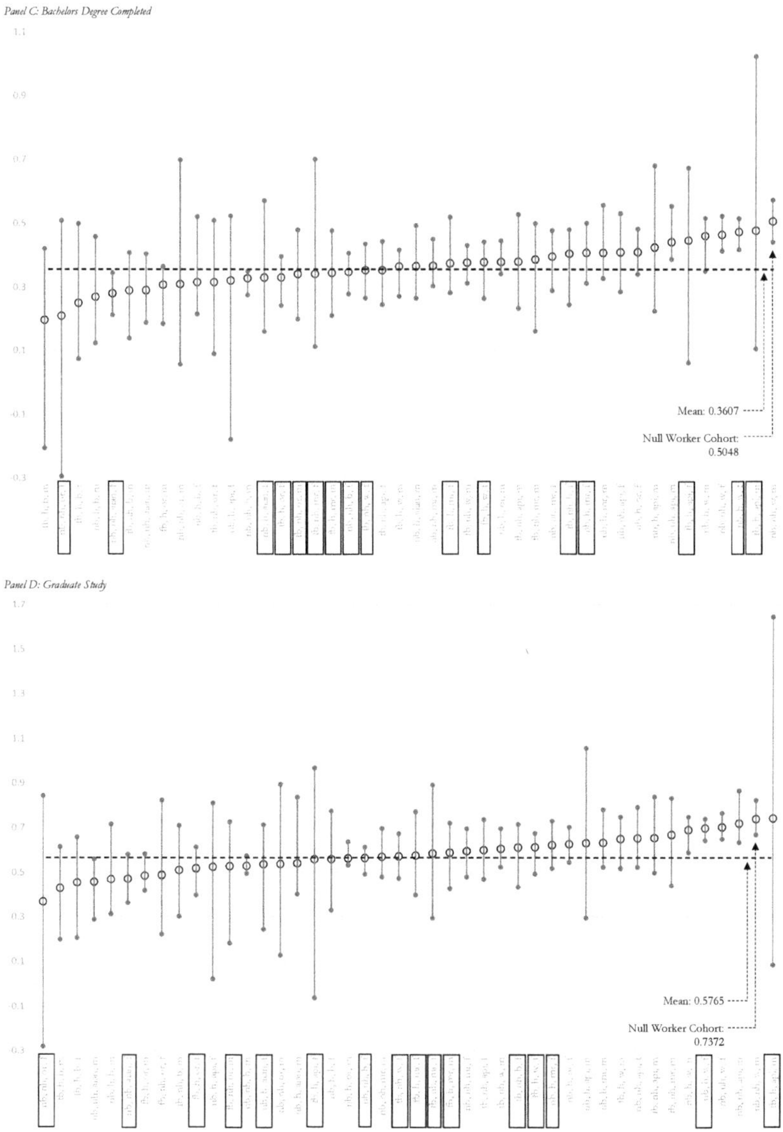

Fig. 5.2 (continued)

Consistent with the values illustrated in Fig. 5.1, across all four panels of Fig. 5.2, we see considerable variation in average estimated returns to education; however, in all four panels, we find no clear relationships between intersectional wage discrimination and pre-market discrimination that manifests through lower returns to educational attainment. As in Fig. 5.1, on the x-axis, boxes have been placed around the labels for each of the 16 worker groups that are reported in Table 5.2 to experience intersectional wage discrimination. Regardless of the level of educational attainment that is considered, there are no statistically significant differences in the mean values for returns to educational attainment between the worker groups that experience intersectional wage discrimination and those that do not. Further, the differences in mean values range from 0.0036 for the "some college" level of educational attainment to 0.0195 for the "high school graduates" level of attainment.

Finally, with respect to personal characteristics, we see considerable variation in returns to years of education and returns to educational attainment. Further, this variation and the patterns that have been identified are consistent with the notion that workers with certain personal characteristics may experience pre-market discrimination and, consequently, realize lesser returns to schooling as compared to workers with different personal characteristics.

Additional relevant information is presented in Fig. 5.3. The figure presents four scatterplots, one for each of the four education classifications for which we examined average returns to schooling in Fig. 5.2. For each of the educational attainment classifications, we plot each worker group's returns to educational attainment against their average estimated discrimination rate. Additionally, for each scatterplot, we include a line of best fit and note the corresponding pairwise correlation coefficient value and whether the value is statistically significant from zero.

We see that, regardless of education classification, a negative relationship is found between worker group-specific average returns to schooling and average estimated discrimination rates. For all classifications except the completion of a four-year college degree, the correlation coefficients are both negative and statistically significant from zero. These findings illustrate that worker groups for which higher average discrimination rates generally have lower average estimated returns to education values. Again, while this is not direct evidence of pre-market discrimination, the information gleaned from our review of returns to education—whether calculated as returns to years of schooling or returns to specific levels of

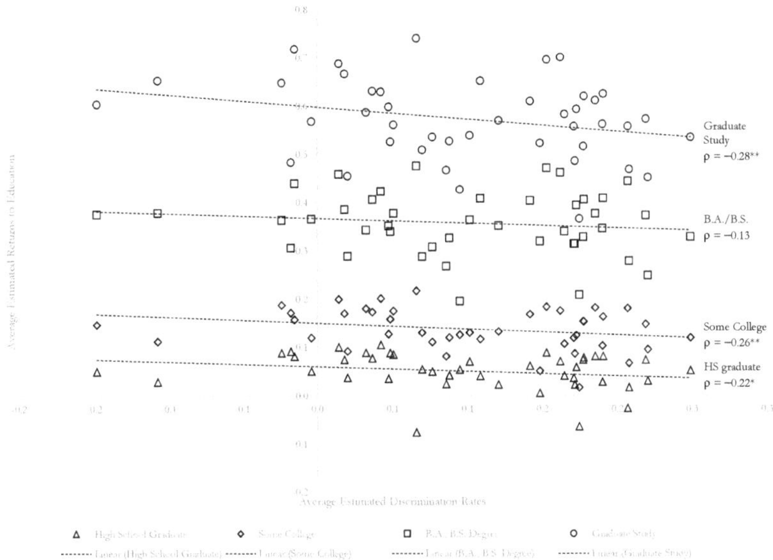

Fig. 5.3 Relationships between average estimated discrimination rates and average estimated returns to education, by educational attainment category (*Note* Average values for all series are calculated across all coefficient estimates regardless of statistical significance from zero. "***', "**", and "*" denote statistical significance from zero (i.e., linear independence) at the 1%, 5%, and 10% levels of significance)

educational attainment—coupled with the average estimated discrimination rates presented in the previous chapter is consistent with pre-market discrimination related to education.

5.3 A Summary

Building on the material presented in earlier chapters, we have addressed the important question of whether wage discrimination is intersectional (i.e., non-additive). We have also considered the existence of pre-labor market discrimination by examining differences in returns to schooling across worker groups and by evaluating the relationships between average estimated discrimination rates and returns to schooling across levels of educational attainment. For the majority of worker groups examined, we report findings that strongly suggest wage discrimination is, in fact, intersectional.

Examining worker groups for which statistically significant evidence of wage discrimination is reported in Chapter 4, we find that expected and estimated discrimination rates vary by more than five percentage points in most instances. This is an important finding for several reasons. First, we extend the literature by reporting evidence in support of Crenshaw's notion of intersectional wage discrimination. This suggests that intersectional analysis should be employed, to the extent that data allow, to examine labor market inequities more completely. Second, our finding of intersectional wage discrimination is consistent with the results of prior studies that have examined more-narrowly defined worker groups (i.e., that are based on fewer personal characteristics). Third, given that we have considered four personal characteristics and, thus, a correspondingly large number of worker groups, our results allow for a more detailed consideration of patterns of wage discrimination across multiple intersecting identities. With respect to pre-market discrimination, while our results are not definitive, we do not report findings that are consistent with a relationship between pre-market discrimination and intersectional wage discrimination.

Appendix

Table 5.3 Returns to years of education (Eq. 3.9)

Worker group	*2008*	*2009*	*2010*	*2011*	*2012*	*2013*	*2014*
fb, h, api, f	0.0502	0.0777	0.0254	0.0684	b	b	0.0373
fb, h, api, m	b	0.0216	0.0820	b	0.0269	0.0131	0.0578
fb, h, b, f	0.0410	0.0377	0.0532	0.0273	0.0474	0.0266	0.0256
fb, h, b, m	0.0217	0.0205	0.0175	0.0367	0.0185	0.0445	0.0242
fb, h, mr, f	0.0284	0.0298	0.0162	0.0396	0.0315	0.0305	0.0293
fb, h, mr, m	0.0167	0.0209	0.0299	0.0187	0.0247	0.0235	0.0324
fb, h, or, f	0.0195	0.0246	0.0279	0.0306	0.0290	0.0275	0.0272
fb, h, or, m	0.0164	0.0202	0.0251	0.0222	0.0227	0.0203	0.0238
fb, h, w, f	0.0284	0.0336	0.0375	0.0378	0.0378	0.0369	0.0383
fb, h, w, m	0.0237	0.0243	0.0298	0.0274	0.0307	0.0301	0.0307
fb, nh, api, f	0.0406	0.0422	0.0502	0.0463	0.0571	0.0494	0.0502
fb, nh, api, m	0.0412	0.0464	0.0461	0.0509	0.0509	0.0578	0.0557
fb, nh, b, f	0.0409	0.0551	0.0499	0.0666	0.0568	0.0558	0.0516
fb, nh, b, m	0.0285	0.0366	0.0351	0.0475	0.0550	0.0431	0.0445
fb, nh, mr, f	0.0269	0.0340	0.0619	0.0717	0.0523	0.0294	0.0446
fb, nh, mr, m	0.0439	0.0366	0.0340	0.0591	0.0579	0.0517	0.0454
fb, nh, or, f	0.0551	0.0279	0.0295	0.0565	0.0592	0.0361	0.0354
fb, nh, or, m	0.0369	0.0578	0.0421	0.0495	0.0184	0.0387	0.0392
fb, nh, w, f	0.0514	0.0567	0.0613	0.0628	0.0696	0.0626	0.0666
fb, nh, w, m	0.0536	0.0636	0.0575	0.0553	0.0600	0.0575	0.0605
nb, h, aian, f	0.0510	0.0757	0.0578	0.0482	0.0628	0.0426	0.0432
nb, h, aian, m	0.0256	0.0327	0.0410	0.0473	0.0518	0.0237	0.0362
nb, h, api, f	0.1062	0.0721	0.1127	0.0925	0.0784	0.0809	0.0961
nb, h, api, m	0.0430	0.0784	0.0456	0.0865	0.0488	0.0292	0.0553
nb, h, b, f	0.0688	0.0605	0.0637	0.0569	0.0936	0.0590	0.0557
nb, h, b, m	0.0378	0.0600	0.0309	0.0327	0.0554	0.0312	0.0401

(continued)

Table 5.3 (continued)

Worker group	*2008*	*2009*	*2010*	*2011*	*2012*	*2013*	*2014*
nb, h, mr, f	0.0558	0.0637	0.0862	0.0662	0.0743	0.0540	0.0591
nb, h, mr, m	0.0427	0.0421	0.0567	0.0603	0.0601	0.0550	0.0469
nb, h, or, f	0.0589	0.0697	0.0695	0.0633	0.0628	0.0543	0.0647
nb, h, or, m	0.0390	0.0437	0.0431	0.0420	0.0446	0.0405	0.0410
nb, h, w, f	0.0703	0.0793	0.0799	0.0771	0.0827	0.0717	0.0758
nb, h, w, m	0.0534	0.0623	0.0643	0.0667	0.0678	0.0597	0.0598
nb, nh, aian, f	0.0599	0.0510	0.0525	0.0613	0.0541	0.0619	0.0645
nb, nh, aian, m	0.0487	0.0504	0.0298	0.0416	0.0469	0.0375	0.0360
nb, nh, api, f	0.0722	0.0855	0.0774	0.0743	0.0788	0.0789	0.0803
nb, nh, api, m	0.0734	0.0752	0.0835	0.0858	0.0868	0.0730	0.0799
nb, nh, b, f	0.0584	0.0748	0.0717	0.0714	0.0743	0.0718	0.0710
nb, nh, b, m	0.0451	0.0535	0.0522	0.0520	0.0564	0.0528	0.0551
nb, nh, mr, f	0.0710	0.0685	0.0656	0.0800	0.0727	0.0901	0.0742
nb, nh, mr, m	0.0594	0.0553	0.0646	0.0666	0.0631	0.0694	0.0659
nb, nh, or, f	0.0514	0.0459	0.0771	0.0437	0.0541	0.0467	0.0379
nb, nh, or, m	0.0560	0.0306	0.0540	0.0510	0.0810	0.0459	0.0473
nb, nh, w, f	0.0826	0.0912	0.0911	0.0913	0.0930	0.0890	0.0903
nb, nh, w, m	0.0758	0.0826	0.0827	0.0839	0.0836	0.0809	0.0820

Worker group	*2015*	*2016*	*2017*	*2018*	*2019*	*2020*
fb, h, api, f	b	0.0297	b	0.0969	b	0.0495
fb, h, api, m	0.0322	0.0403	b	0.0018	0.0364	0.0881
fb, h, b, f	0.0279	0.0290	0.0518	0.0325	0.0256	0.0184
fb, h, b, m	0.0097	0.0227	0.0281	0.0451	0.0275	0.0170
fb, h, mr, f	0.0332	0.0307	0.0431	0.0493	0.0459	0.0398
fb, h, mr, m	0.0216	0.0315	0.0261	0.0292	0.0386	0.0338
fb, h, or, f	0.0230	0.0219	0.0251	0.0240	0.0238	0.0199
fb, h, or, m	0.0193	0.0176	0.0285	0.0188	0.0234	0.0157
fb, h, w, f	0.0386	0.0367	0.0390	0.0367	0.0383	0.0424
fb, h, w, m	0.0301	0.0305	0.0271	0.0329	0.0356	0.0350
fb, nh, api, f	0.0543	0.0507	0.0517	0.0633	0.0623	0.0545
fb, nh, api, m	0.0549	0.0582	0.0550	0.0736	0.0691	0.0552
fb, nh, b, f	0.0615	0.0540	0.0592	0.0631	0.0686	0.0551
fb, nh, b, m	0.0394	0.0484	0.0409	0.0655	0.0439	0.0431
fb, nh, mr, f	0.0480	0.0651	0.0556	0.0716	0.0874	0.0549
fb, nh, mr, m	0.0651	0.0558	0.0602	0.0716	0.0587	0.0670
fb, nh, or, f	0.0450	0.0316	0.0359	0.0507	0.0401	0.0405
fb, nh, or, m	0.0453	0.0201	0.0141	0.0382	0.0288	0.0545
fb, nh, w, f	0.0666	0.0617	0.0622	0.0711	0.0738	0.0780
fb, nh, w, m	0.0622	0.0560	0.0569	0.0691	0.0727	0.0693
nb, h, aian, f	0.0383	0.0556	0.0640	0.0754	0.0590	0.0525

(continued)

Table 5.3 (continued)

Worker group	*2015*	*2016*	*2017*	*2018*	*2019*	*2020*
nb, h, aian, m	0.0379	0.0493	0.0304	0.0540	0.0482	0.0477
nb, h, api, f	0.0242	0.0378	0.0560	0.0331	0.0284	0.0569
nb, h, api, m	0.0759	0.0614	0.0492	0.1076	0.0297	0.0501
nb, h, b, f	0.0348	0.0591	0.0784	0.0841	0.0569	0.0460
nb, h, b, m	0.0599	0.0466	0.0300	0.0437	0.0369	0.0540
nb, h, mr, f	0.0629	0.0710	0.0599	0.0691	0.0661	0.0751
nb, h, mr, m	0.0420	0.0463	0.0597	0.0688	0.0623	0.0597
nb, h, or, f	0.0555	0.0541	0.0515	0.0613	0.0521	0.0450
nb, h, or, m	0.0455	0.0426	0.0384	0.0411	0.0357	0.0371
nb, h, w, f	0.0724	0.0697	0.0710	0.0777	0.0782	0.0672
nb, h, w, m	0.0573	0.0603	0.0561	0.0645	0.0617	0.0506
nb, nh, aian, f	0.0461	0.0660	0.0514	0.0524	0.0575	0.0631
nb, nh, aian, m	0.0369	0.0461	0.0390	0.0410	0.0556	0.0387
nb, nh, api, f	0.0802	0.0748	0.0819	0.0896	0.0925	0.1157
nb, nh, api, m	0.0700	0.0834	0.0807	0.0910	0.0910	0.0909
nb, nh, b, f	0.0675	0.0696	0.0693	0.0731	0.0776	0.0661
nb, nh, b, m	0.0552	0.0531	0.0543	0.0593	0.0557	0.0504
nb, nh, mr, f	0.0847	0.0812	0.0799	0.0870	0.0913	0.0918
nb, nh, mr, m	0.0671	0.0680	0.0644	0.0735	0.0804	0.0685
nb, nh, or, f	0.0369	0.0315	0.0425	0.0513	0.0640	0.0412
nb, nh, or, m	0.0636	0.0138	0.0582	0.0680	0.0542	0.0450
nb, nh, w, f	0.0898	0.0907	0.0920	0.0981	0.0970	0.0937
nb, nh, w, m	0.0823	0.0833	0.0842	0.0944	0.0915	0.0893

Table 5.4 Returns to levels of educational attainment (Eq. 3.12)

Panel A: High school diploma

Worker Group	*2008*	*2009*	*2010*	*2011*	*2012*	*2013*	*2014*
fb, h, api, f	−0.4074	−0.0009	−0.3757	−0.0775	b	b	0.3533
fb, h, api, m	b	−0.3469	0.2990	b	0.0421	−0.3044	−0.1520
fb, h, b, f	0.0370	0.0358	0.0792	0.1477	0.0494	0.0946	−0.0072
fb, h, b, m	0.0699	0.1261	0.0536	0.1073	0.0240	−0.0223	0.0612
fb, h, mr, f	0.0276	0.0700	0.0498	0.2151	0.0442	0.0676	0.0767
fb, h, mr, m	0.0224	0.1252	0.1119	0.0678	0.1035	0.0620	0.1286
fb, h, or, f	0.0635	0.0588	0.0990	0.0846	0.0826	0.1154	0.0885
fb, h, or, m	0.0814	0.0736	0.1221	0.0855	0.0998	0.0981	0.1166
fb, h, w, f	0.0587	0.0873	0.0971	0.1218	0.0883	0.1053	0.0671
fb, h, w, m	0.0790	0.0638	0.1053	0.0919	0.1059	0.0942	0.1020
fb, nh, api, f	0.0186	0.0464	0.0881	0.0305	0.1057	0.0073	0.0187
fb, nh, api, m	0.0252	0.0046	0.0084	0.0515	0.0423	0.0549	0.0421
fb, nh, b, f	0.0316	0.0513	0.0962	0.1101	0.1035	0.0492	0.0645
fb, nh, b, m	0.0031	0.0640	0.0384	0.1106	0.0859	0.0527	0.0705
fb, nh, mr, f	0.0033	−0.0052	−0.0137	0.1095	0.0954	0.0913	0.0156
fb, nh, mr, m	0.1812	−0.0141	−0.0060	0.1412	0.1967	0.0505	0.0834
fb, nh, or, f	0.0702	−0.1120	0.1158	0.1138	0.2036	0.1001	0.0328
fb, nh, or, m	0.1314	0.0205	0.1026	0.1169	0.1098	0.1891	0.1445
fb, nh, w, f	0.0200	0.0478	0.0453	0.0036	0.0919	0.0465	0.0088
fb, nh, w, m	0.0682	0.1005	0.0459	0.0278	0.0513	0.0612	0.0537
nb, h, aian, f	−0.0257	0.1457	0.1537	−0.1950	0.1719	0.0911	−0.0301
nb, h, aian, m	0.0011	0.0261	0.1120	0.1700	0.0848	0.2098	−0.0279
nb, h, api, f	−0.0157	0.1442	−0.0938	0.1507	0.1184	−0.0435	0.1065
nb, h, api, m	−0.1050	0.1306	0.3585	−0.0818	−0.0338	0.0363	0.2306

(continued)

Table 5.4 (continued)

Panel A: High school diploma

Worker Group	*2008*	*2009*	*2010*	*2011*	*2012*	*2013*	*2014*
nb, h, b, f	0.0187	0.0716	0.0581	0.0093	−0.0370	−0.0006	−0.0051
nb, h, b, m	0.0618	0.1963	0.0111	0.0534	0.0015	0.0093	−0.0099
nb, h, mr, f	0.1565	0.1219	0.1131	0.0288	0.0822	−0.0110	0.0033
nb, h, mr, m	0.0871	0.0593	0.1150	0.1049	0.0561	0.0903	0.0799
nb, h, or, f	0.1002	0.0919	0.1036	0.0996	0.1006	0.0896	0.1196
nb, h, or, m	0.0875	0.1116	0.0893	0.0940	0.0779	0.0664	0.0630
nb, h, w, f	0.1028	0.0789	0.1025	0.1086	0.1016	0.1044	0.0765
nb, h, w, m	0.1046	0.1154	0.1238	0.1110	0.0929	0.1118	0.1011
nb, nh, aian, f	0.0562	0.0054	0.0316	−0.0302	0.0071	0.0212	0.0285
nb, nh, aian, m	0.0499	0.0901	−0.0403	0.0352	0.0769	0.0589	0.0247
nb, nh, api, f	−0.0139	0.1630	0.0686	0.0569	0.0491	−0.0138	−0.1045
nb, nh, api, m	0.1152	0.0488	0.0630	0.0579	0.0481	0.1295	0.0489
nb, nh, b, f	0.0486	0.0453	0.0506	0.0455	0.0679	0.0222	0.0238
nb, nh, b, m	0.0324	0.0700	0.0418	0.0497	0.0681	0.0520	0.0462
nb, nh, mr, f	0.1316	0.0895	0.0856	0.0948	0.0223	−0.0105	0.1026
nb, nh, mr, m	0.0552	0.0611	0.0500	0.0646	0.0645	0.0312	0.0947
nb, nh, or, f	0.1726	0.1031	0.1445	−0.0353	−0.3702	0.0256	−0.6740
nb, nh, or, m	−0.0114	−0.0668	0.2014	0.1212	0.2155	0.1673	0.1520
nb, nh, w, f	0.0753	0.0963	0.0870	0.0894	0.0829	0.0637	0.0578
nb, nh, w, m	0.0980	0.1159	0.1081	0.1097	0.1095	0.1096	0.1146

Panel A: High school diploma

Worker Group	*2015*	*2016*	*2017*	*2018*	*2019*	*2020*
fb, h, api, f	b	0.3726	b	−0.1492	b	0.0768
fb, h, api, m	−0.1348	−0.0429	b	−0.0850	−0.0743	0.0402
fb, h, b, f	0.0753	−0.0009	0.1374	−0.0124	−0.0445	−0.1962
fb, h, b, m	−0.0930	0.0615	0.2111	0.0466	0.1460	−0.0931
fb, h, mr, f	0.0861	0.0533	0.0372	0.0861	0.0566	0.0897
fb, h, mr, m	0.0689	0.1078	0.1024	0.1005	0.0742	0.0759
fb, h, or, f	0.0772	0.0548	0.0802	0.0715	0.0560	0.0309
fb, h, or, m	0.0757	0.0645	0.1149	0.0799	0.0982	0.0731
fb, h, w, f	0.0616	0.0840	0.0669	0.0880	0.0634	0.0716
fb, h, w, m	0.0943	0.0893	0.0915	0.0716	0.0852	0.0707
fb, nh, api, f	0.0319	0.0249	0.0244	0.0148	0.0518	−0.0087
fb, nh, api, m	0.0569	0.0328	0.0265	0.0774	0.0137	−0.0636
fb, nh, b, f	0.0314	0.0551	0.0784	0.0597	0.0674	−0.0035
fb, nh, b, m	0.0032	0.0957	0.0427	0.0958	0.0341	0.0115
fb, nh, mr, f	−0.0592	0.1790	0.0893	−0.0198	0.1848	−0.1351
fb, nh, mr, m	0.0309	0.1326	0.0809	0.0093	0.0457	0.0308
fb, nh, or, f	0.1103	−0.0182	−0.0153	0.0625	−0.3260	−0.0420
fb, nh, or, m	−0.0012	−0.0342	0.0597	0.1641	0.0498	0.0952
fb, nh, w, f	0.0357	−0.0585	−0.0285	0.0072	0.0632	0.0113
fb, nh, w, m	0.0613	0.0464	0.0266	0.0370	0.0309	0.0357
nb, h, aian, f	0.0213	0.0677	0.1565	0.1273	0.0611	−0.0709

(continued)

Table 5.4 (continued)

Panel A: High school diploma

Worker Group	*2015*	*2016*	*2017*	*2018*	*2019*	*2020*
nb, h, aian, m	0.1332	0.0761	0.0543	0.0308	0.0447	0.0011
nb, h, api, f	−0.0110	−0.1034	0.2577	−0.0719	−0.4411	0.0712
nb, h, api, m	0.2265	0.1996	0.0962	0.2424	0.2277	−0.1618
nb, h, b, f	−0.0579	0.0092	0.2345	0.1646	−0.0080	0.0194
nb, h, b, m	0.0693	−0.0416	−0.0402	−0.0189	0.0617	−0.0462
nb, h, mr, f	0.1612	0.1490	0.0854	0.0200	0.0392	0.0719
nb, h, mr, m	0.0378	0.0127	0.0680	0.1357	0.0926	0.0661
nb, h, or, f	0.0377	0.0614	0.0738	0.0489	0.0797	0.0549
nb, h, or, m	0.1325	0.0969	0.0833	0.0726	0.0620	0.0657
nb, h, w, f	0.0777	0.0735	0.0902	0.0872	0.0784	0.0703
nb, h, w, m	0.1062	0.1063	0.0863	0.1138	0.1037	0.0220
nb, nh, aian, f	−0.0243	0.0861	0.0119	−0.0490	0.0430	0.0304
nb, nh, aian, m	0.0522	0.0383	0.0409	−0.0047	0.0508	0.0087
nb, nh, api, f	0.1062	0.0780	0.0680	0.0751	−0.0548	0.0498
nb, nh, api, m	0.0973	0.0573	0.1057	0.1314	0.1185	0.0259
nb, nh, b, f	0.0222	0.0170	0.0243	0.0189	−0.0025	−0.0176
nb, nh, b, m	0.0400	0.0372	0.0491	0.0328	0.0204	0.0012
nb, nh, mr, f	0.0219	−0.0551	0.0821	0.0626	0.0799	0.0583
nb, nh, mr, m	0.0778	0.0575	−0.0079	0.0331	0.0542	0.0159
nb, nh, or, f	0.3138	−0.0630	−0.1709	−0.0221	−0.0518	−0.1997
nb, nh, or, m	−0.0169	−0.1854	−0.0046	0.1398	−0.0054	−0.0589
nb, nh, w, f	0.0598	0.0529	0.0588	0.0579	0.0844	0.0590

Panel A: High school diploma

Worker Group	*2015*	*2016*	*2017*	*2018*	*2019*	*2020*
nb, nh, w, m	0.1036	0.1035	0.0980	0.1120	0.1101	0.0994

Panel B: Some college

Worker Group	*2008*	*2009*	*2010*	*2011*	*2012*	*2013*	*2014*
fb, h, api, f	−0.1254	0.7185	−0.0957	0.0615	b	b	0.3380
fb, h, api, m	b	−0.0742	0.6501	b	0.4964	0.2183	0.3335
fb, h, b, f	0.1747	0.1283	0.2263	0.2146	0.0902	0.0949	0.0555
fb, h, b, m	0.1507	0.1266	0.1609	0.1621	−0.0001	0.0560	0.2467
fb, h, mr, f	0.1331	0.1451	0.0938	0.2085	0.0811	0.1136	0.1369
fb, h, mr, m	0.0825	0.1691	0.2323	0.1652	0.2380	0.1944	0.2593
fb, h, or, f	0.1242	0.1484	0.2047	0.1644	0.1845	0.1764	0.1822
fb, h, or, m	0.1238	0.1800	0.1864	0.1868	0.1877	0.1809	0.1920
fb, h, w, f	0.1444	0.1733	0.1936	0.2144	0.2162	0.1844	0.1831
fb, h, w, m	0.1460	0.1542	0.1938	0.1905	0.2148	0.2016	0.1997
fb, nh, api, f	0.1044	0.1116	0.1854	0.1398	0.2164	0.1207	0.1116
fb, nh, api, m	0.0892	0.0833	0.0872	0.1317	0.1217	0.1535	0.1259
fb, nh, b, f	0.1004	0.1503	0.1941	0.2228	0.2071	0.1754	0.1781
fb, nh, b, m	0.0370	0.1404	0.1168	0.2008	0.1610	0.1445	0.1300
fb, nh, mr, f	0.0696	−0.0022	0.1496	0.1751	0.1910	0.1047	0.0939
fb, nh, mr, m	0.2300	−0.0161	0.0889	0.2698	0.3271	0.2576	0.0874
fb, nh, or, f	0.2408	−0.1339	0.0444	0.2823	0.1263	0.1486	0.0734
fb, nh, or, m	0.1479	0.2730	0.1314	0.3015	0.2609	0.2548	0.2288

(continued)

Table 5.4 (continued)

Panel B: Some college

Worker Group	*2008*	*2009*	*2010*	*2011*	*2012*	*2013*	*2014*
fb, nh, w, f	0.1081	0.1543	0.1653	0.1125	0.1976	0.1549	0.1081
fb, nh, w, m	0.1353	0.1796	0.1492	0.1412	0.1404	0.1576	0.1410
nb, h, aian, f	0.1111	0.2856	0.2384	−0.1301	0.1717	0.1392	0.0687
nb, h, aian, m	0.0670	0.1126	0.2048	0.0864	0.1280	0.2211	−0.0067
nb, h, api, f	−0.0063	0.2067	0.0028	0.2190	0.1720	0.0573	0.2305
nb, h, api, m	0.0838	0.1768	0.4328	0.2811	0.0689	0.1699	0.3950
nb, h, b, f	0.1421	0.1406	0.1332	0.1179	0.0594	0.0756	0.0809
nb, h, b, m	0.1614	0.2424	0.0343	0.0362	0.0461	0.0253	0.0796
nb, h, mr, f	0.1932	0.2200	0.1413	0.0821	0.2355	0.0742	0.0949
nb, h, mr, m	0.1655	0.1262	0.1589	0.1726	0.2175	0.1593	0.1392
nb, h, or, f	0.1836	0.1769	0.1636	0.2152	0.2043	0.1608	0.2114
nb, h, or, m	0.1808	0.2033	0.1897	0.1880	0.1991	0.1463	0.1704
nb, h, w, f	0.1764	0.1828	0.2151	0.2000	0.2154	0.1983	0.1779
nb, h, w, m	0.1817	0.2080	0.2228	0.2017	0.2154	0.2223	0.2090
nb, nh, aian, f	0.1092	0.0545	0.0908	0.0665	0.0610	0.0576	0.0939
nb, nh, aian, m	0.1231	0.1176	0.0137	0.0887	0.1114	0.1100	0.1019
nb, nh, api, f	0.0669	0.2633	0.1192	0.1061	0.1245	0.1126	0.0114
nb, nh, api, m	0.1954	0.1338	0.1703	0.1798	0.1242	0.2031	0.1761
nb, nh, b, f	0.1155	0.1151	0.1387	0.1300	0.1532	0.0984	0.1068
nb, nh, b, m	0.1068	0.1560	0.1228	0.1241	0.1509	0.1323	0.1229
nb, nh, mr, f	0.1791	0.1471	0.1572	0.1548	0.0955	0.0837	0.1548
nb, nh, mr, m	0.1057	0.1322	0.1385	0.1324	0.1316	0.0939	0.1578
nb, nh, or, f	0.1881	0.1756	0.2645	0.0663	−0.1488	0.1034	−0.5380

Panel B: Some college

Worker Group	*2008*	*2009*	*2010*	*2011*	*2012*	*2013*	*2014*
nb, nh, or, m	0.1583	−0.0704	0.1857	−0.0051	0.4940	0.1425	0.2405
nb, nh, w, f	0.1644	0.1974	0.1962	0.2012	0.1854	0.1692	0.1626
nb, nh, w, m	0.1939	0.2150	0.2129	0.2147	0.2168	0.2074	0.2161

Panel B: Some college

Worker Group	*2015*	*2016*	*2017*	*2018*	*2019*	*2020*
fb, h, api, f	b	0.3537	b	−0.0884	b	0.2876
fb, h, api, m	−0.0221	0.0389	b	−0.2061	0.3158	0.4237
fb, h, b, f	0.0823	0.0409	0.1228	0.0990	−0.0470	−0.0402
fb, h, b, m	0.0448	0.0547	0.2258	0.1933	0.2129	0.0040
fb, h, mr, f	0.2180	0.1916	0.1143	0.1576	0.2021	0.1356
fb, h, mr, m	0.1321	0.2218	0.1728	0.1792	0.1328	0.1683
fb, h, or, f	0.1345	0.1360	0.1520	0.1478	0.1496	0.1041
fb, h, or, m	0.1666	0.1507	0.1948	0.1530	0.1811	0.1510
fb, h, w, f	0.1713	0.1973	0.1689	0.1789	0.1656	0.1805
fb, h, w, m	0.2007	0.1940	0.1623	0.1855	0.2050	0.1919
fb, nh, api, f	0.1038	0.1101	0.0986	0.1215	0.1579	0.0736
fb, nh, api, m	0.1413	0.1065	0.1135	0.1608	0.1346	0.0093
fb, nh, b, f	0.1130	0.1464	0.1694	0.1993	0.1836	0.1546
fb, nh, b, m	0.0670	0.1671	0.1404	0.2140	0.0943	0.0783
fb, nh, mr, f	0.0218	0.1210	0.1577	0.0076	0.2752	0.0282
fb, nh, mr, m	0.1507	0.1712	0.1459	0.1853	0.1781	0.1418

(continued)

Table 5.4 (continued)

Panel B: Some college

Worker Group	*2015*	*2016*	*2017*	*2018*	*2019*	*2020*
fb, nh, or, f	0.1214	−0.0136	0.1448	0.1270	−0.1895	0.1569
fb, nh, or, m	0.2388	0.0161	0.1286	0.1034	−0.1513	0.1302
fb, nh, w, f	0.1288	0.0625	0.0639	0.1445	0.1861	0.1378
fb, nh, w, m	0.1588	0.1513	0.1152	0.1539	0.1400	0.1439
nb, h, aian, f	0.0488	0.1005	0.2491	0.0696	0.1741	0.0307
nb, h, aian, m	0.2144	0.2379	0.0459	0.1290	0.1228	0.1297
nb, h, api, f	−0.0999	0.0530	0.2253	−0.1579	−0.3504	0.1104
nb, h, api, m	0.2140	0.2484	0.1935	0.3053	0.1304	−0.0763
nb, h, b, f	0.0199	0.0406	0.3099	0.2177	0.0974	0.1161
nb, h, b, m	0.1251	0.0168	−0.0378	0.0439	0.1494	0.1327
nb, h, mr, f	0.2290	0.2119	0.1832	0.0793	0.1045	0.1537
nb, h, mr, m	0.1495	0.1377	0.1881	0.2814	0.1986	0.1646
nb, h, or, f	0.1130	0.1494	0.1296	0.1257	0.1600	0.1355
nb, h, or, m	0.2020	0.1959	0.1712	0.1515	0.1307	0.1550
nb, h, w, f	0.1777	0.1780	0.1709	0.1796	0.1752	0.1465
nb, h, w, m	0.2151	0.2046	0.1912	0.2253	0.1898	0.1127
nb, nh, aian, f	0.0103	0.1232	0.0365	−0.0395	0.1424	0.0665
nb, nh, aian, m	0.0916	0.0821	0.0856	0.0400	0.1439	0.0834
nb, nh, api, f	0.1682	0.1248	0.1329	0.1519	0.0296	0.1064
nb, nh, api, m	0.1220	0.1156	0.1802	0.2121	0.1748	0.0616
nb, nh, b, f	0.0906	0.0943	0.0929	0.0938	0.0733	0.0391
nb, nh, b, m	0.1126	0.1054	0.1286	0.1227	0.0967	0.0782
nb, nh, mr, f	0.1017	0.0056	0.1542	0.1251	0.1488	0.1152

Panel B: Some college

Worker Group	*2015*	*2016*	*2017*	*2018*	*2019*	*2020*
nb, nh, mr, m	0.1233	0.1072	0.0733	0.1062	0.1518	0.1000
nb, nh, or, f	0.2506	−0.0543	−0.1125	0.0308	0.0972	−0.1053
nb, nh, or, m	0.0292	−0.1176	0.0841	0.2757	0.0412	−0.0183
nb, nh, w, f	0.1623	0.1507	0.1541	0.1814	0.2006	0.1698
nb, nh, w, m	0.2025	0.2106	0.2052	0.2377	0.2272	0.2176

Panel C: B.A./B.S. Degree

Worker Group	*2008*	*2009*	*2010*	*2011*	*2012*	*2013*	*2014*
fb, h, api, f	−0.1254	0.7185	−0.0957	0.0615	b	b	0.3380
fb, h, api, m	b	−0.0742	0.6501	b	0.4964	0.2183	0.3335
fb, h, b, f	0.1747	0.1283	0.2263	0.2146	0.0902	0.0949	0.0555
fb, h, b, m	0.1507	0.1266	0.1609	0.1621	−0.0001	0.0560	0.2467
fb, h, mr, f	0.1331	0.1451	0.0938	0.2085	0.0811	0.1136	0.1369
fb, h, mr, m	0.0825	0.1691	0.2323	0.1652	0.2380	0.1944	0.2593
fb, h, or, f	0.1242	0.1484	0.2047	0.1644	0.1845	0.1764	0.1822
fb, h, or, m	0.1238	0.1800	0.1864	0.1868	0.1877	0.1809	0.1920
fb, h, w, f	0.1444	0.1733	0.1936	0.2144	0.2162	0.1844	0.1831
fb, h, w, m	0.1460	0.1542	0.1938	0.1905	0.2148	0.2016	0.1997
fb, nh, api, f	0.1044	0.1116	0.1854	0.1398	0.2164	0.1207	0.1116
fb, nh, api, m	0.0892	0.0833	0.0872	0.1317	0.1217	0.1535	0.1259
fb, nh, b, f	0.1004	0.1503	0.1941	0.2228	0.2071	0.1754	0.1781
fb, nh, b, m	0.0370	0.1404	0.1168	0.2008	0.1610	0.1445	0.1300

(continued)

Table 5.4 (continued)

Panel C: B.A./B.S. Degree

Worker Group	*2008*	*2009*	*2010*	*2011*	*2012*	*2013*	*2014*
fb, nh, mr, f	0.0696	−0.0022	0.1496	0.1751	0.1910	0.1047	0.0939
fb, nh, mr, m	0.2300	−0.0161	0.0889	0.2698	0.3271	0.2576	0.0874
fb, nh, or, f	0.2408	−0.1339	0.0444	0.2823	0.1263	0.1486	0.0734
fb, nh, or, m	0.1479	0.2730	0.1314	0.3015	0.2609	0.2548	0.2288
fb, nh, w, f	0.1081	0.1543	0.1653	0.1125	0.1976	0.1549	0.1081
fb, nh, w, m	0.1353	0.1796	0.1492	0.1412	0.1404	0.1576	0.1410
nb, h, aian, f	0.1111	0.2856	0.2384	−0.1301	0.1717	0.1392	0.0687
nb, h, aian, m	0.0670	0.1126	0.2048	0.0864	0.1280	0.2211	−0.0067
nb, h, api, f	−0.0063	0.2067	0.0028	0.2190	0.1720	0.0573	0.2305
nb, h, api, m	0.0838	0.1768	0.4328	0.2811	0.0689	0.1699	0.3950
nb, h, b, f	0.1421	0.1406	0.1332	0.1179	0.0594	0.0756	0.0809
nb, h, b, m	0.1614	0.2424	0.0343	0.0362	0.0461	0.0253	0.0796
nb, h, mr, f	0.1932	0.2200	0.1413	0.0821	0.2355	0.0742	0.0949
nb, h, mr, m	0.1655	0.1262	0.1589	0.1726	0.2175	0.1593	0.1392
nb, h, or, f	0.1836	0.1769	0.1636	0.2152	0.2043	0.1608	0.2114
nb, h, or, m	0.1808	0.2033	0.1897	0.1880	0.1991	0.1463	0.1704
nb, h, w, f	0.1764	0.1828	0.2151	0.2000	0.2154	0.1983	0.1779
nb, h, w, m	0.1817	0.2080	0.2228	0.2017	0.2154	0.2223	0.2090
nb, nh, aian, f	0.1092	0.0545	0.0908	0.0665	0.0610	0.0576	0.0939
nb, nh, aian, m	0.1231	0.1176	0.0137	0.0887	0.1114	0.1100	0.1019
nb, nh, api, f	0.0669	0.2633	0.1192	0.1061	0.1245	0.1126	0.0114
nb, nh, api, m	0.1954	0.1338	0.1703	0.1798	0.1242	0.2031	0.1761
nb, nh, b, f	0.1155	0.1151	0.1387	0.1300	0.1532	0.0984	0.1068

Panel C: B.A./B.S. Degree

Worker Group	*2008*	*2009*	*2010*	*2011*	*2012*	*2013*	*2014*
nb, nh, b, m	0.1068	0.1560	0.1228	0.1241	0.1509	0.1323	0.1229
nb, nh, mr, f	0.1791	0.1471	0.1572	0.1548	0.0955	0.0837	0.1548
nb, nh, mr, m	0.1057	0.1322	0.1385	0.1324	0.1316	0.0939	0.1578
nb, nh, or, f	0.1881	0.1756	0.2645	0.0663	−0.1488	0.1034	−0.5380
nb, nh, or, m	0.1583	−0.0704	0.1857	−0.0051	0.4940	0.1425	0.2405
nb, nh, w, f	0.1644	0.1974	0.1962	0.2012	0.1854	0.1692	0.1626
nb, nh, w, m	0.1939	0.2150	0.2129	0.2147	0.2168	0.2074	0.2161

Panel C: B.A./B.S. degree

Worker Group	*2015*	*2016*	*2017*	*2018*	*2019*	*2020*
fb, h, api, f	b	0.3537	b	−0.0884	b	0.2876
fb, h, api, m	−0.0221	0.0389	b	−0.2061	0.3158	0.4237
fb, h, b, f	0.0823	0.0409	0.1228	0.0990	−0.0470	−0.0402
fb, h, b, m	0.0448	0.0547	0.2258	0.1933	0.2129	0.0040
fb, h, mr, f	0.2180	0.1916	0.1143	0.1576	0.2021	0.1356
fb, h, mr, m	0.1321	0.2218	0.1728	0.1792	0.1328	0.1683
fb, h, or, f	0.1345	0.1360	0.1520	0.1478	0.1496	0.1041
fb, h, or, m	0.1666	0.1507	0.1948	0.1530	0.1811	0.1510
fb, h, w, f	0.1713	0.1973	0.1689	0.1789	0.1656	0.1805
fb, h, w, m	0.2007	0.1940	0.1623	0.1855	0.2050	0.1919
fb, nh, api, f	0.1038	0.1101	0.0986	0.1215	0.1579	0.0736
fb, nh, api, m	0.1413	0.1065	0.1135	0.1608	0.1346	0.0093

(continued)

Table 5.4 (continued)

Panel C: B.A./B.S. degree

Worker Group	*2015*	*2016*	*2017*	*2018*	*2019*	*2020*
fb, nh, b, f	0.1130	0.1464	0.1694	0.1993	0.1836	0.1546
fb, nh, b, m	0.0670	0.1671	0.1404	0.2140	0.0943	0.0783
fb, nh, mr, f	0.0218	0.1210	0.1577	0.0076	0.2752	0.0282
fb, nh, mr, m	0.1507	0.1712	0.1459	0.1853	0.1781	0.1418
fb, nh, or, f	0.1214	−0.0136	0.1448	0.1270	−0.1895	0.1569
fb, nh, or, m	0.2388	0.0161	0.1286	0.1034	−0.1513	0.1302
fb, nh, w, f	0.1288	0.0625	0.0639	0.1445	0.1861	0.1378
fb, nh, w, m	0.1588	0.1513	0.1152	0.1539	0.1400	0.1439
nb, h, aian, f	0.0488	0.1005	0.2491	0.0696	0.1741	0.0307
nb, h, aian, m	0.2144	0.2379	0.0459	0.1290	0.1228	0.1297
nb, h, api, f	−0.0999	0.0530	0.2253	−0.1579	−0.3504	0.1104
nb, h, api, m	0.2140	0.2484	0.1935	0.3053	0.1304	−0.0763
nb, h, b, f	0.0199	0.0406	0.3099	0.2177	0.0974	0.1161
nb, h, b, m	0.1251	0.0168	−0.0378	0.0439	0.1494	0.1327
nb, h, mr, f	0.2290	0.2119	0.1832	0.0793	0.1045	0.1537
nb, h, mr, m	0.1495	0.1377	0.1881	0.2814	0.1986	0.1646
nb, h, or, f	0.1130	0.1494	0.1296	0.1257	0.1600	0.1355
nb, h, or, m	0.2020	0.1959	0.1712	0.1515	0.1307	0.1550
nb, h, w, f	0.1777	0.1780	0.1709	0.1796	0.1752	0.1465
nb, h, w, m	0.2151	0.2046	0.1912	0.2253	0.1898	0.1127
nb, nh, aian, f	0.0103	0.1232	0.0365	−0.0395	0.1424	0.0665
nb, nh, aian, m	0.0916	0.0821	0.0856	0.0400	0.1439	0.0834
nb, nh, api, f	0.1682	0.1248	0.1329	0.1519	0.0296	0.1064

Panel C: B.A./B.S. degree

Worker Group	*2015*	*2016*	*2017*	*2018*	*2019*	*2020*
nb, nh, api, m	0.1220	0.1156	0.1802	0.2121	0.1748	0.0616
nb, nh, b, f	0.0906	0.0943	0.0929	0.0938	0.0733	0.0391
nb, nh, b, m	0.1126	0.1054	0.1286	0.1227	0.0967	0.0782
nb, nh, mr, f	0.1017	0.0056	0.1542	0.1251	0.1488	0.1152
nb, nh, mr, m	0.1233	0.1072	0.0733	0.1062	0.1518	0.1000
nb, nh, or, f	0.2506	−0.0543	−0.1125	0.0308	0.0972	−0.1053
nb, nh, or, m	0.0292	−0.1176	0.0841	0.2757	0.0412	−0.0183
nb, nh, w, f	0.1623	0.1507	0.1541	0.1814	0.2006	0.1698
nb, nh, w, m	0.2025	0.2106	0.2052	0.2377	0.2272	0.2176

Panel D: Graduate Study

Worker Group	*2008*	*2009*	*2010*	*2011*	*2012*	*2013*	*2014*
fb, h, api, f	0.0608	0.5698	0.1813	0.5905	b	b	0.4274
fb, h, api, m	b	0.1177	1.0232	b	0.7012	0.2738	0.4955
fb, h, b, f	0.3336	0.2906	0.4979	0.2998	0.3481	0.3117	0.1078
fb, h, b, m	0.1243	0.0338	0.1204	0.3481	0.2669	0.4193	0.2592
fb, h, mr, f	0.3432	0.3683	0.2987	0.5179	0.2810	0.3989	0.3334
fb, h, mr, m	0.2096	0.3042	0.3269	0.2667	0.2823	0.3513	0.4008
fb, h, or, f	0.2418	0.2852	0.3886	0.3759	0.3680	0.3296	0.3948
fb, h, or, m	0.1842	0.2416	0.3545	0.2886	0.3288	0.3123	0.3634
fb, h, w, f	0.2636	0.3691	0.3754	0.3877	0.3815	0.3809	0.3893
fb, h, w, m	0.2706	0.3008	0.3627	0.3576	0.3736	0.3743	0.3857

(continued)

Table 5.4 (continued)

Panel D: Graduate Study

Worker Group	*2008*	*2009*	*2010*	*2011*	*2012*	*2013*	*2014*
fb, nh, api, f	0.2442	0.2739	0.3776	0.3515	0.4309	0.3359	0.3451
fb, nh, api, m	0.2329	0.2925	0.3139	0.3682	0.3669	0.4097	0.4001
fb, nh, b, f	0.2437	0.3854	0.4189	0.4792	0.4433	0.3863	0.3954
fb, nh, b, m	0.1379	0.2405	0.2541	0.3639	0.3840	0.3077	0.2960
fb, nh, mr, f	0.1670	0.1117	0.3590	0.5265	0.3346	0.2770	0.3763
fb, nh, mr, m	0.4103	0.1606	0.1865	0.4463	0.4937	0.3792	0.3530
fb, nh, or, f	0.4188	0.1307	0.2745	0.4745	0.3989	0.2758	0.3702
fb, nh, or, m	0.2802	0.2632	0.3170	0.4786	0.4134	0.3152	0.3294
fb, nh, w, f	0.2648	0.3312	0.3586	0.3176	0.4290	0.3762	0.3446
fb, nh, w, m	0.3115	0.3785	0.3582	0.3392	0.3475	0.3971	0.3902
nb, h, aian, f	0.1594	0.5695	0.4499	0.1896	0.3710	0.2049	0.3072
nb, h, aian, m	0.3083	0.2640	0.4673	0.3864	0.2855	0.3484	0.2702
nb, h, api, f	0.4688	0.4276	0.4769	0.5214	0.3503	0.4498	0.4475
nb, h, api, m	0.4803	0.4093	0.5304	0.5604	0.2575	0.2727	0.3067
nb, h, b, f	0.3455	0.3091	0.3798	0.3100	0.2678	0.2641	0.2852
nb, h, b, m	0.3063	0.4572	0.1937	0.2363	0.2960	0.1229	0.2264
nb, h, mr, f	0.4132	0.4469	0.4120	0.3290	0.4891	0.3114	0.3190
nb, h, mr, m	0.3376	0.3260	0.4241	0.4458	0.4532	0.4241	0.3497
nb, h, or, f	0.4223	0.4810	0.4311	0.4691	0.4302	0.4095	0.4555
nb, h, or, m	0.3409	0.4047	0.3845	0.3522	0.4071	0.3838	0.3472
nb, h, w, f	0.4498	0.4699	0.4997	0.5056	0.5137	0.4731	0.4643
nb, h, w, m	0.4286	0.4601	0.4669	0.4824	0.4834	0.4814	0.4644
nb, nh, aian, f	0.2992	0.2857	0.2538	0.3250	0.2599	0.2552	0.2868

Panel D: Graduate Study

Worker Group	*2008*	*2009*	*2010*	*2011*	*2012*	*2013*	*2014*
nb, nh, aian, m	0.2996	0.4030	0.1881	0.2698	0.3536	0.2977	0.2186
nb, nh, api, f	0.3042	0.5292	0.3809	0.3932	0.3914	0.3768	0.2842
nb, nh, api, m	0.3955	0.3870	0.4392	0.4114	0.4103	0.4586	0.4796
nb, nh, b, f	0.3062	0.3570	0.3757	0.3818	0.4047	0.3399	0.3570
nb, nh, b, m	0.2740	0.3439	0.3330	0.3350	0.3487	0.3379	0.3278
nb, nh, mr, f	0.4092	0.3547	0.4036	0.4262	0.3223	0.3434	0.4087
nb, nh, mr, m	0.3020	0.3416	0.3679	0.3652	0.3581	0.3256	0.4099
nb, nh, or, f	0.3393	0.3448	0.5072	0.1560	0.1317	0.1475	−0.2955
nb, nh, or, m	0.2207	0.0562	0.3050	0.2861	0.6980	0.1970	0.4364
nb, nh, w, f	0.4125	0.4685	0.4707	0.4698	0.4625	0.4432	0.4457
nb, nh, w, m	0.4399	0.4900	0.4880	0.4993	0.4968	0.4886	0.5047

Panel D: Graduate study

Worker Group	*2015*	*2016*	*2017*	*2018*	*2019*	*2020*
fb, h, api, f	b	0.6731	b	0.5251	b	0.5299
fb, h, api, m	0.3547	0.4087	b	0.1047	0.3985	0.8834
fb, h, b, f	0.1919	0.1238	0.3791	0.0933	0.0732	0.1895
fb, h, b, m	0.0727	0.1602	0.2615	0.3114	0.3767	−0.2058
fb, h, mr, f	0.3694	0.3498	0.3603	0.4470	0.4149	0.3700
fb, h, mr, m	0.3824	0.4158	0.2824	0.3554	0.4755	0.4101
fb, h, or, f	0.3079	0.3069	0.3712	0.3479	0.2838	0.2761
fb, h, or, m	0.3013	0.2691	0.3573	0.3088	0.3385	0.3323

(continued)

Table 5.4 (continued)

Panel D: Graduate study

Worker Group	*2015*	*2016*	*2017*	*2018*	*2019*	*2020*
fb, h, w, f	0.3925	0.3899	0.3715	0.3803	0.3792	0.4403
fb, h, w, m	0.3999	0.3673	0.3375	0.3765	0.4030	0.4150
fb, nh, api, f	0.3522	0.3413	0.3174	0.4101	0.4423	0.3510
fb, nh, api, m	0.4108	0.3804	0.3875	0.5268	0.4901	0.3397
fb, nh, b, f	0.3758	0.3827	0.4060	0.4490	0.4663	0.4164
fb, nh, b, m	0.2153	0.3429	0.2780	0.4068	0.2450	0.2752
fb, nh, mr, f	0.2618	0.5125	0.2932	0.2161	0.7000	0.2874
fb, nh, mr, m	0.3905	0.4231	0.4337	0.4497	0.4976	0.3869
fb, nh, or, f	0.5079	0.0968	0.2791	0.4563	0.0893	0.3193
fb, nh, or, m	0.4456	0.1984	0.2129	0.4151	0.3500	0.3997
fb, nh, w, f	0.3598	0.2836	0.2901	0.3771	0.4342	0.4066
fb, nh, w, m	0.4117	0.3599	0.3203	0.4222	0.4293	0.4165
nb, h, aian, f	0.1674	0.3730	0.4558	0.4261	0.3346	0.2663
nb, h, aian, m	0.4909	0.4581	0.2703	0.3487	0.4263	0.4077
nb, h, api, f	0.1292	0.2789	0.4873	−0.0024	−0.1788	0.2987
nb, h, api, m	0.5501	0.3430	0.5451	0.6803	0.2240	0.3465
nb, h, b, f	0.2148	0.2223	0.5195	0.4615	0.2727	0.2392
nb, h, b, m	0.4092	0.2660	0.1509	0.2196	0.2944	0.3087
nb, h, mr, f	0.4989	0.4747	0.4133	0.3338	0.3968	0.4427
nb, h, mr, m	0.3488	0.3433	0.3855	0.5549	0.4442	0.4451
nb, h, or, f	0.3685	0.3594	0.3391	0.3974	0.3854	0.3662
nb, h, or, m	0.4437	0.3938	0.3689	0.3581	0.3478	0.3757
nb, h, w, f	0.4693	0.4527	0.4605	0.4853	0.4731	0.4163

Panel D: Graduate study

Worker Group	*2015*	*2016*	*2017*	*2018*	*2019*	*2020*
nb, h, w, m	0.4570	0.4608	0.4421	0.5145	0.4790	0.3492
nb, nh, aian, f	0.2369	0.3431	0.2285	0.2123	0.3428	0.2997
nb, nh, aian, m	0.2823	0.3085	0.2924	0.2340	0.3680	0.2417
nb, nh, api, f	0.4530	0.4044	0.4094	0.5034	0.3823	0.4925
nb, nh, api, m	0.3857	0.4359	0.4692	0.5527	0.4978	0.3975
nb, nh, b, f	0.3384	0.3306	0.3406	0.3533	0.3403	0.2769
nb, nh, b, m	0.3281	0.3200	0.3355	0.3481	0.3130	0.3014
nb, nh, mr, f	0.3867	0.2878	0.4314	0.4317	0.4759	0.4440
nb, nh, mr, m	0.3593	0.3608	0.3105	0.4181	0.4490	0.3852
nb, nh, or, f	0.3827	0.1570	0.0633	0.3555	0.3829	0.0466
nb, nh, or, m	0.2908	0.0667	0.3515	0.5298	0.3537	0.2141
nb, nh, w, f	0.4463	0.4395	0.4492	0.5011	0.5215	0.4844
nb, nh, w, m	0.4920	0.4996	0.4999	0.5711	0.5555	0.5371

Note b = too few observations

References

Kim, Marlene. 2009. Race and Gender Differences in the Earnings of Black Workers. *Industrial Relations* 48 (3): 466–488.

George, Erin E, Jessica Milli, and Sophie Tripp. 2022. Worse than a Double Whammy: The Intersectional Causes of Wage Inequality between Women of Colour and White Men Over time. *Labour* 36 (3): 302–341.

Paul, Mark, Khaing Zaw, and William Darity. 2022. Returns in the Labor Market: A Nuanced View of Penalties at the Intersection of Race and Gender in the US. *Feminist Economics* 28 (2): 1–31.

CHAPTER 6

A Summary and Concluding Thoughts

Abstract We close with a summary that discusses our topic, the corresponding research questions, and the methodology and empirical strategy we have employed. We then summarize our results and emphasize the importance of considering intersectionality when examining wage discrimination. Lastly, we revisit the motivation for this work, returning to the topics of social justice and economic justice. We stress that episodes of inequitable treatment can have significant negative impacts on an individual and, by extension, on society. Likewise, persistent and widespread disparate treatment in labor market outcomes can be devastating for an individual and corrosive to a society.

Keywords Conclusions · Empirical strategy · Justice · Research questions · Summary

In our initial chapter, we introduced economic justice as a dimension of social justice. We then presented wage discrimination as a form of economic injustice and thus, by extension, an example of social injustice. From that starting point, we presented evidence of persistent differences in unemployment rates and hourly wage differentials across race- and sex-based classifications, respectively. We then presented unadjusted wage gaps (i.e., raw differences in average hourly wage rates) for a number of

R. White, *Intersectionality and Discrimination*,
https://doi.org/10.1007/978-3-031-26125-1_6

broadly defined worker groups that represent the non-productive personal characteristics we consider during our study. These characteristics include Hispanic ethnicity, nativity, race, and sex. This led to a discussion of intersectionality and our primary research question: Is wage discrimination intersectional? This is followed by an explanation for why we use the term "discrimination" when referring to differences in wage rates that cannot be explained by differences in workers' productive characteristics.

To provide context for our study, in Chapter 2, we presented a detailed non-technical introduction to the two dominant economic theories of labor market discrimination (i.e., taste-based discrimination and statistical discrimination). We discussed the emotional motives for taste-based discrimination, including individual-level and contextual-level explanations for intergroup bias. In our discussion of statistical discrimination, we emphasized how imperfect information can lead a rational, profit-seeking employer to discriminate. Specifically, we focused on how experiences, generalizations, and stereotypes may lead to discrimination if employers find it difficult or impossible to predict the productivity of a potential hire or to accurately measure the productivities of existing employees. Having provided theoretical rationale for the existence of wage discrimination, we reviewed the related economic literature and closed the chapter by explicitly stating our full set of research questions: (1) Is wage discrimination additive or non-additive (i.e., intersectional)? (2) Does observed wage discrimination vary across worker groups and, if so, does the variation follow a pattern(s) that suggests the discrimination is intersectional? and (3) Do we find evidence of a relationship between pre-labor market wage discrimination with respect to the returns to schooling and intersectional wage discrimination?

Sandwiched between the introduction of our research questions and the presentation of our results, we detailed the methodology we use to examine wage discrimination. This included a derivation of the Mincer earnings function, which is the foundation for the battery of regression models that we estimate, and discussions of the Blinder-Oaxaca decomposition technique and the Heckman sample selection model, both of which are essential to our empirical strategy. To demonstrate our methodology, we presented results obtained from a series of preliminary estimations and subsequent decompositions. Our preliminary estimations compared a cohort of white male workers, separately, to three worker groups that were comprised of white female, black male, and black female workers. In each instance, significant portions of the respective wage gaps could not be explained by differences in productive characteristics; thus, the estimations were consistent with the presence of wage discrimination.

Building on our initial findings, we examined annual data for the period from 2008 through 2020 to produce annual estimates of wage discrimination for each of the 43 worker groups that are defined based on unique combinations of the workers' personal characteristics of Hispanic ethnicity, nativity, race, and sex. In the typical year during our 2008–2020 reference period, we examine data for 882,342 workers, and over our entire reference period, we examine data for 11,470,451 workers. Given that we estimate four regression models for each of our 43 worker groups for each of the 13 years in our reference period, in total, we produce more than 2,200 estimates of wage discrimination.

To answer our primary research question, we compare our estimated discrimination rates to expected discrimination rates. For a given worker group, the estimated discrimination rate is the sum of personal characteristic-specific discrimination rates. The personal characteristic-specific discrimination rates are obtained by comparing each worker group that differs from our null worker cohort of native-born, non-Hispanic, white, male workers in two or more personal characteristics to another worker group that differs by a single characteristic. If for a given worker group, the expected discrimination rate is within five percentage points of the estimated discrimination rate, we conclude that the wage discrimination is additive. Finally, as a modest application of our findings, we consider possible evidence of pre-labor market discrimination by considering variation across worker groups in average returns to education with the identification of intersectional wage discrimination.

Our estimates of wage discrimination rates vary considerably across worker groups. Examination of data for the year 2020 reveals positive discrimination rate estimates that are statistically significant from zero for 30 of the 43 worker groups. Among these 30 worker groups, the average estimated discrimination rates across our four regression models range in value from 2.49% (for the native-born, non-Hispanic, Asian or Pacific Islander, male worker group) to 27.34% (for the foreign-born, Hispanic, black, female worker group). Twenty-two of these 30 groups include female workers (73.3%). While Hispanic workers are included in only 16 of the 30 groups, they are included in eight of the 10 groups with the highest average estimated discrimination rates. Similarly, although foreign-born workers are included in only 14 of the 30 groups, they are found six times among the seven highest average estimated discrimination rates. These general frequencies and patterns are also found when looking at earlier years in our reference period.

When addressing our first research question, we conclude that average estimated wage discrimination rates vary, often considerably so, across worker groups and that groups with higher average estimated discrimination rates are frequently comprised of female, Hispanic, and/or foreign-born workers. While these results are interesting and informative, they neither support nor refute the notion that wage discrimination is intersectional.

To determine whether wage discrimination is intersectional, we calculate expected discrimination rates and compare the expected rates to our estimated discrimination rates. Examining worker groups that differ from the null cohort of native-born, non-Hispanic, white, male workers in two or more of the four personal characteristics we consider and for which statistically significant evidence of wage discrimination is reported, we find that expected and estimated discrimination rates vary by more than five percentage points in the majority of cases. We consider this to be strong evidence that wage discrimination is, in fact, intersectional for many of the worker groups we consider.

Our final research question involves pre-labor market discrimination that is related to education and that may affect workers' subsequent wages. When estimating our regression models to identify potential wage discrimination, we also obtain estimates of the returns to schooling for each year examined, each regression model estimated, and every worker group considered. We examine differences in estimated returns to schooling across worker groups, and we evaluate the relationship between average estimated discrimination rates and returns to schooling across levels of educational attainment. Across our four educational attainment classifications, we compare worker group-specific average estimated discrimination rates to corresponding average estimated returns to education. We find, regardless of education classification, that the worker groups with higher average estimated discrimination rates generally have lower average returns to education. However, we find no compelling evidence of a statistical relationship between pre-labor market wage discrimination with respect to the returns to schooling and intersectional wage discrimination.

Even though we have addressed a series of important questions and produced information that extends the collective knowledge on intersectional wage discrimination in the U.S. labor market, there is much more that remains to be discovered. We have examined worker groups defined by combinations of four personal characteristics. A more complete analysis would also consider potential wage discrimination related to other legally protected characteristics (i.e., age [i.e., 40 years and older], disability, national origin, religion, gender identity, sexual orientation, etc.). A more expansive analysis would consider a lengthier reference period and/or would extend beyond wage discrimination to include discrimination in hiring and other forms of labor market discrimination.

Progress in any of these areas would lead to a more thorough empirical understanding of labor market discrimination. More complete and accurate information may aid in the formulation of related public policies. Likewise, since discrimination is not without significant economic, psychological, and social costs, more and better information may lead individuals to rethink the consequences of their biases and prejudices and whether to engage in discrimination. If additional knowledge can change undesirable behaviors, then we may realize more equitable labor market outcomes. If so, there is a direct benefit in terms of enhanced economic justice and, accordingly, greater social justice.

As we have noted, the contributions presented here are modest relative to what would be ideal and to the full extent of what is needed to eliminate wage discrimination. This is acknowledged. Our hope, however, is that the information provided here is a step toward more just and equitable labor market outcomes. In closing, we revisit the first paragraph of our initial chapter in which it is made clear that wage discrimination can be quite harmful for an individual. The elimination of wage discrimination is potentially transformative. It may allow a worker to earn a living wage, have access to a quality education and affordable childcare, and be able to afford a roof over their head and food for their family. In a few words, greater economic justice is important at a societal level and it is as important, and most likely more so, at the individual level.

Index

R. White, *Intersectionality and Discrimination*,
https://doi.org/10.1007/978-3-031-26125-1

GPSR Compliance
The European Union's (EU) General Product Safety Regulation (GPSR) is a set of rules that requires consumer products to be safe and our obligations to ensure this.

If you have any concerns about our products, you can contact us on

ProductSafety@springernature.com

In case Publisher is established outside the EU, the EU authorized representative is:

Springer Nature Customer Service Center GmbH
Europaplatz 3
69115 Heidelberg, Germany

www.ingramcontent.com/pod-product-compliance
Ingram Content Group UK Ltd.
Pitfield, Milton Keynes, MK11 3LW, UK
UKHW020836290926
15470UKWH00004B/1383

9783031261244